There are more than 1,000 Chinese churches in the USA now and the number is still increasing! Research is needed to understand the rise and influence of this emergent group and this book is a significant contribution to this understanding. Combining quantitative and qualitative methods, Jeanne Wu articulates convincingly how Chinese churches in the USA do mission in a globalized world. With clear theoretical framework and missiological insights, it will be a critical support to the advance of diaspora missiology.

Joy Kooi-Chin Tong, PhD
Author of *Overseas Chinese Christian Entrepreneurs in Modern China:*
A Case Study of Christian Ethics on Business Life
Professor, Sociology Department & Center on Religion and Chinese Society,
Purdue University, Indiana, USA

Mission through Diaspora is a carefully researched and well-written work which deals with a subject of considerable contemporary significance – the Chinese diaspora movement and its involvement in mission. Jeanne Wu bases her work upon careful research, not simply anecdotal reports, and brings significant personal experience to the study, which is reflected in her observations and recommendations. This is an original and important contribution to our understanding of global Christianity and contemporary missions.

Harold A. Netland, PhD
Editor of *Globalizing Theology: Belief and Practice in an Era of World Christianity*
Professor of Philosophy of Religion and Intercultural Studies,
Trinity Evangelical Divinity School, Deerfield, Illinois, USA

I0128529

Mission through Diaspora

The Case of the Chinese Church in the USA

Jeanne Wu

Langham

MONOGRAPHS

© 2016 by Jeanne Wu

Published 2016 by Langham Monographs
an imprint of Langham Creative Projects

Langham Partnership
PO Box 296, Carlisle, Cumbria CA3 9WZ, UK
www.langham.org

ISBNs:
978-1-78368-109-9 Print
978-1-78368-864-7 Mobi
978-1-78368-178-5 ePub
978-1-78368-179-2 PDF

British Library Cataloguing in Publication Data
A catalogue record for this book is available from the British Library

ISBN: 978-1-78368-109-9

Cover & Book Design: projectluz.com

To the Chinese church in the USA

Contents

LIST OF FIGURES

LIST OF TABLES

Acknowledgments

I am grateful for the wisdom and encouragement from my mentor, Dr Bob Priest, the love and care of my husband, Scott, and the support in various ways from the Chinese churches in the USA. Without them I could not have finished my studies. *Soli Deo Gloria*!

CHAPTER 1

Introduction

"Diaspora Mission" and "Diaspora Missiology" have become popular terminology recently among missiologists. Diaspora was included on the
agenda of the Third Lausanne Congress in Cape Town in 2010, during
which the Lausanne Global Diaspora Network Advisory Board was formed.
The Evangelical Missiology Society (EMS) chose "Diaspora Missiology" as
the national theme in 2014. Diaspora missiology raises questions such as,
"Who is moving?" "Why are they moving?" and "How does their movement impact mission work?" In the article, "Diaspora Missiology," Enoch
Wan provides statistical data to identify the moving people groups, and
the "push" and "pull" factors that move people.[1] These moving people
can be immigrants, visitors, students, workers, or refugees. Wan calls diaspora missiology "mission on our doorstep,"[2] meaning that we can reach
different people groups in our neighborhood (especially in the US context). Samuel Escobar, in his article "Migration: Avenue and Challenge
to Mission,"[3] suggests the similar notion that "migration is an avenue for
the evangelistic dimension of mission." Escobar observes that migrants are
people in transition and uncertainty, and thus "such people in transition
are open to become believers, ready to assume a faith in a personal way."[4] A
good example is the large amount of conversions of mainland Chinese in
the United States. From both sociological and psychological perspectives,

---

1. Enoch Wan, "Diaspora Missiology," *EMS*, Occasional Bulletin (2007): 3–7.

2. Ibid.

3. Samuel Escobar, "Migration: Avenue and Challenge to Mission," *Missiology* 31,
no. 1 (2003): 19.

4. Ibid.

Christianity meets their needs and answers their questions in the midst of this transition.[5]

But diaspora mission is more than outreach to migrants; it can also be mission *by* diaspora. In the Chinese context, "overseas Chinese" have more religious resources and freedom than Chinese people in China, and therefore the Chinese mission movement is predominantly carried out by Chinese diaspora. As Wan concludes in his study, the numerical data shows two missiological trends of Chinese diaspora: "the emergence of both mission opportunities among them and the potentials in mission participation by them."[6]

Wan further summarizes these strategies and practices of diaspora missions as "missions to the diaspora," "missions through the diaspora," and "missions by and beyond diaspora."[7] Missions to the diaspora is mission which reaches out to new immigrants or migrants such as international students or workers; missions through the diaspora refers to new immigrants or migrants reaching out to their kinsmen in their country of origin or other countries; missions by and beyond diaspora is cross-cultural mission done by diaspora reaching out to people who are not their kinsmen.

Chinese Christians and church leaders have often observed that Chinese churches in the US invest their resources mainly in missions related to Chinese ministries, whether long-term or short-term mission. In the article, "It Is Time to Reflect: Rethink the Mission Strategy of Chinese Church," Tsu-Kung Chuang, a senior pastor of a Chinese church on the East Coast, provides several examples of overseas Chinese doing missions to Chinese, commenting that it is common that overseas Chinese churches spend most of their mission budget on Chinese missions.[8] Furthermore,

---

5. Fenggang Yang, "Chinese Conversion to Evangelical Christianity: The Importance of Social and Cultural Contexts," *Sociology of Religion* 59 (1998); Yuting Wang and Fenggang Yang, "More Than Evangelical and Ethnic: The Ecological Factor in Chinese Conversion to Christianity in the United States," *Sociology of Religion* 67, no. 2 (2006).

6. Enoch Wan, "Mission among the Chinese Diaspora: A Case Study of Migration & Mission," *Missiology* XXXI, no. 1 (2003): 38.

7. Enoch Wan, ed., *Diaspora Missiology: Theory, Methodology, and Practice* (Portland, OR: Institute of Diaspora Studies-USA, 2011), 138–140.

8. Tsu-Kung Chuang, "It Is Time to Reflect: Rethink the Mission Strategy of Chinese Church," (該是檢討的時候了——華人教會宣教策略的省思) . *Church China* (教會), issue 8, November 2007. https://www.churchchina.org/?q=no071101.

many US Chinese churches organize their own short-term mission trips regularly, and the majority of their short-term mission trips, in short, are from Chinese diaspora to Chinese nationals in mainland China and/or to Chinese diaspora in other parts of the world. In the article, "Chinese Christian Transnationalism: Diverse Networks of a Houston Church," Fenggang Yang observes the diverse transnational ties of Chinese Christian congregations through his field research in Houston, Taiwan, Hong Kong and mainland China. The members of US Chinese churches are mainly from Taiwan, Hong Kong, mainland China and Southeast Asia, and the church and its members maintain these transnational ties. This is done through individuals and organizations, such as supporting ministries or missionaries abroad, as well as families and friends.[9] This kind of trans-national network opens the door for US Chinese churches to carry out short-term missions overseas. We may call this kind of practice "short-term mission as transnationalism."

Zephaniah Yu, the director of the Chinese mission agency Gospel Operation International, wrote an article regarding the strategy of Chinese mission.[10] He lists four stages of missions from his perspective (examples are added):

> (I) "Local Local" – missions to a people group of the same culture in the same place (e.g. Chinese Christians in Chicago reaching out to new Chinese immigrants in Chicago).

> (II) "Local Global" – missions to a people group of near or different culture in the same place (e.g. Chinese Christians in Chicago reaching out to new Indonesian immigrants in Chicago).

> (III) "Global Local" – missions to a people group of the same or near culture in different places (e.g. Chinese Christians in Chicago reaching out to Chinese who live in Germany).

---

9. Fenggang Yang, "Chinese Christian Transnationalism: Diverse Networks of a Houston Church," in *Religions across Borders: Transnational Religious Networks*, eds. Helen Rose Ebaugh and Janet S. Chafetz (Walnut Creek, CA: AltaMira, 2002).

10. Zephaniah T. C. Yu, "From the End of Earth to Our Neighbor (從天涯至毗鄰)," *Gospel Operation International* (華傳) 23 (Sept–Oct 2013).

(IV) "Global Global" – missions to a people group of different cultures in different places (e.g. Chinese Christians in Chicago reaching out to Indonesians in Indonesia).

Yu's model of different stages of mission is similar to the "E-1," "E-2" and "E-3" model developed by Ralph Winter:

E-1: Evangelism of people outside the church but within one's culture. Only one barrier is crossed: the "stained-glass" membership boundaries of the church.

E-2: Evangelism of people of different but similar cultures. Two barriers are crossed: The "stained-glass" barrier and an additional cultural distance sufficient to require separate church fellowships.

E-3: Evangelism of people of radically different cultures. To emphasize the greater cultural distance of an evangelist attempting to communicate to a radically different and potentially hostile environment, it is supposed that evangelists attempt to cross at least three barriers in E-3 efforts.[11]

These models can be seen as inspired by Acts 1:8 – "And you will be my witnesses in Jerusalem, and in all Judea and Samaria, and to the ends of the earth." The Chinese churches in the USA normally practice (I) "Local Local" and (III) "Global Local." In terms of diaspora missiology, (I) and (III) correspond to "missions through diaspora," and (II) and (IV) are "mission by/beyond diaspora."[12] Yu further explains that the vision and emphasis of their mission agency has been (III) "Global Local" for the past eighteen years, and their goal is to move forward to (IV) "Global Global." One of their strategies is to educate and mobilize the Chinese Christians for (IV) missions by practicing (II) "Local Global."[13] This progressional way of thinking about mission can be helpful in explaining the typical Chinese way of doing missions. Gospel Operation International's goal and vision of

---

11. Ralph D. Winter and Steve C. Hawthorne, *Perspectives on the World Christian Movement* (Pasadena, CA: William Carey Library, 1999), 64.

12. (II) can be "mission to diaspora" if the local Christians are non-diaspora, e.g. Americans reaching out to Indonesians in Chicago.

13. Yu, "From the End of Earth," 2.

missions represents the general situation of overseas Chinese churches: they currently invest most of their resources in the ministries to Chinese people in the same place and different places, while also recognizing that their mission is not yet completely reflecting the Great Commission of Jesus Christ, which is to "be my witnesses . . . to the ends of the earth."

The current study examines the practice of "missions through diaspora" by studying the mission practice – especially self-organized short-term mission trips – of Chinese churches in the United States. With little to no difference in culture and language, Chinese Christians in the USA are able to minister to other Chinese effectively and directly. This is different from the short-term missions conducted by Americans of European ancestry. One example, from my own experience, is that many US Chinese churches send short-term mission teams focused on discipleship training to Chinese Christians in mainland China and Europe, while many American Christians focus on construction and related activities on their short-term mission trips.

Most scholars (e.g. Wuthnow and Moreau) define short-term mission as primarily a North American movement, and the literature review in chapter 2 focuses on the short-term mission movement in the USA as well. However, the reality is that many non-Western churches have also been active in short-term mission. Priest mentions in his recent research that Asian, African and Latino churches send out short-term mission teams while also receiving short-term mission teams, and South Korea may even have a higher percentage of Christians involved than in the USA.[14] Stephen Offutt also discusses this trend in his 2011 article, observing that churches in countries like South Africa and El Salvador, which have high Christian populations, both send and receive short-term mission teams. He comments that short-term missions "are helping to diversify international missionary flows and increasing their multidirectional nature."[15]

---

14. Robert J. Priest, "Short-Term Mission as a New Paradigm," in *Mission after Christendom: Emergent Themes in Contemporary Mission*, eds. Ogbu Kalu, Peter Vethanayagamony, and Edmund Kee-Fook Chia (Louisville, KT: Westminster John Knox, 2010), 86.

15. Stephen Offutt, "The Role of Short-Term Mission Teams in the New Centers of Global Christianity," *Journal for the Scientific Study of Religion* 50, no. 4 (2011): 810.

In light of these studies, the present study is intended to examine the short-term mission activity by diaspora Chinese who live in the USA and to compare it with that which is carried out by US megachurches and US Korean churches. In addition to describing the mission practices of the Chinese church, some evaluation on their short-term mission practice will also be made. The tools for evaluation will be biblical revelation as well as past research in short-term missions and diaspora missiology. The primary audiences of this work include short-term missions scholars and practitioners, researchers in diaspora movements and missiology, and Chinese Christians and church leaders in the USA. Such a study has an important contribution to make to our growing understanding of diaspora missiology and the mission practices of the Chinese American church.

Statement of the Research Problem

This research examines the global mission involvements of US Chinese churches, how such involvements connect with global Chinese diaspora communities, and the place of short-term mission in these patterns of global ministry connections. Specifically this research focuses on these three areas:

1) The nature of the mission practice of the US Chinese church and how diaspora theories and diaspora missiology are relevant to this mission practice.

2) The way US Chinese churches conduct short-term mission trips, and how it is similar and/or different in comparison with short-term mission trips of other churches in the United States.

3) The way Chinese Christians in the USA connect and collaborate with other diaspora and national Chinese through short-term mission trips, and how diaspora theories and diaspora missiology are relevant to these collaborative activities.

The research problem covers two major areas related to ethnicity and socio-economics. First, this research examines the mission movement among the US Chinese church – the so-called Chinese diaspora in the USA – studying how the US Chinese church has undertaken short-term mission, and especially how they cooperate with other Chinese diaspora or Chinese nationals. This research is an attempt to test the commonly held notion that Chinese churches tend to invest most of their resources in Chinese ministries, and that short-term missions by Chinese churches are mostly "from Chinese to Chinese." Second, comparison is made with past studies of short-term missions undertaken by general American churches (where the ethnicity is unspecified) and Korean American churches. The hypothesis here is that "the STM activities by Chinese churches in the USA are different from those carried out by American churches which do not specify the ethnicity of the church."

In this research, the following questions are answered: (a) What are the countries to which overseas Chinese churches are sending short-term mission teams? (b) What kind of people are they sending, and with whom are they partnering? (c) How many resources do they invest in short-term mission? (d) What kind of mission work are they doing on the mission field? (e) What is the nature of their relationship with the local people, and how have the participants been impacted by their short-term mission trips? The survey results support both of the aforementioned hypotheses. Furthermore, the diaspora theories, diaspora missiology and the qualitative aspect of this research help elucidate the reasons to explain these phenomena.

Significance of This Study

Chinese diaspora has been well known for its economic activity and capital. For example, Robin Cohen identifies Chinese diaspora as "trade diaspora" in his book *Global Diasporas* (1997). Joy Tong mentions in her book *Overseas Chinese Christian Entrepreneurs in Modern China* that Chinese diaspora have been involved economically in China as early as 1870, during the Qing dynasty.[16] Numerous studies have focused on the economies of overseas Chinese and the rise of the *Nanyang* (Southeast Asia) capitalists,[17] the business and trading relations between overseas Chinese and China,[18] and how *guanxi* (personal relationship and connection) has

---

16. Joy Kooi-Chin Tong, *Overseas Chinese Christian Entrepreneurs in Modern China: A Case Study of Christian Ethics on Business Life* (London: Anthem, 2012), 54.

17. E.g. Michael R. Godley, *The Mandarin-Capitalists from Nanyang* (Cambridge: Cambridge University Press, 1981).

18. E.g. Gungwu Wang, *China and the Chinese Overseas* (Singapore: Times Academic Press, 1991).

played a significant role in Chinese and the overseas Chinese business world.[19] However, studies related to Christianity and mission activities of overseas Chinese are few.[20]

According to the data of the research and development department of Chinese Coordination Centre of World Evangelism (CCCOWE),[21] Chinese diaspora today, with a population of 71 million or more including the Taiwanese population of 23 million, is the largest diaspora in the world (CCCOWE, 2011).[22] Diaspora missiologists suggest that they are not only a people group that needs to be reached, but also can play a strategic role in global missions, especially in ministries to their kinsmen, including the 1.3 billion Chinese in mainland China. According to the data of World Values Surveys, the People's Republic of China is the least religious country among all the countries which have been surveyed: 88.9 percent of Chinese "reported that they never or practically never attended religious services."[23] David Barrett and Todd Johnson divide this world into World A, World B and World C:

> World A: the unevangelized world, where less than 50 percent of people have been evangelized (heard the gospel or heard of Jesus);
>
> World B: the evangelized non-Christian world, where at least 50 percent of people have been evangelized (who have heard, with understanding, about Christianity, Christ, and the

---

19. E.g. Thomas Gold, Doug Guthrie, and David Wank, *Social Connection in China: Institutions, Culture, and the Changing Nature of Guanxi* (Cambridge: Cambridge University Press, 2002).

20. As Tong points out, most studies of this kind makes links with Confucian values (Tong, *Overseas Chinese Christian Entrepreneurs*, 148).

21. https://www.cccowe.org/ (accessed 2 November 2013).

22. CCCOWE published their data of Overseas Chinese population on the quarterly journal Chinese Church. Today in 2011, where they also listed the sources of the data: (1) The 2009 Statistic Report of Overseas Community Affairs Council, Republic of China 《2009 年僑務統計年報》 published in 2010; (2) The data on Chinese in Oceania collected by Chinese Christian Mission New Zealand reported on Handbook of Chinese Missions in Oceania 《大洋洲華人宣教工場手冊大綱》; (3)The data on Chinese in Africa collected and reported by the journal of Gospel Operation International 非洲的百萬華人 《華傳路》 2009, vol. 85.

23. Fenggang Yang, *Religion in China: Survival and Revival under Communist Rule* (New York: Oxford University Press, 2012), 129.

gospel, whether or not they have accepted it or have become disciples of Christ) and less than 60 percent are Christian;

World C: the Christian world – countries that are at least 60 percent Christian (of all kinds, including Roman Catholics, Protestants, Orthodox, Anglicans, Independents and marginal Christians).[24]

Barrett and Johnson report that 13 percent of the world's population belongs to World A, 56 percent to World B and 30 percent to World C. According to this definition, China is listed as the largest World B country with 57.7 percent of the population of their country belonging to World B. On the other hand, the USA is the largest World C country with Christian population of 84.7 percent.[25] This statistical data shows that although China is no longer an "unreached" country, it is still one of the largest mission fields in terms of population.

Currently, research on Chinese mission is comparatively sparse, and most of the articles and books on mission work undertaken by the Chinese church are written in the Chinese language. In addition, although many scholars have researched the short-term mission movement in North America, while others have focused on diaspora missiology, and still others on Chinese diaspora itself, there is no study which connects all three together. Hence, academic research on diaspora Chinese mission is necessary and timely.

Diaspora mission may be an effective mission model, yet it still demands more research to substantiate the theories. The present study is an attempt to interact with the theory of "diaspora missiology." Since the theory, methodology and practice of diaspora missiology are still being formed, it is beneficial to focus on the short-term mission movement of a diaspora group as a way to test these theories and methodologies. Such a study enables us to see the similarities and differences between American short-term mission

---

24. David Barrett and Todd Johnson, *World Christian Trends, AD 30- AD 2200: Interpreting the Annual Christian Megacensus* (Pasadena, CA: William Carey Library, 2001), 761–769.

25. David Barrett, Todd M. Johnson, and Peter F. Crossing, "Missiometrics 2005: A Global Survey of World Mission," *International Bulletin of Missionary Research* 29, no. 1 (2005).

and Chinese diaspora short-term mission, revealing areas of strength as well as growth areas for Chinese diaspora in their kingdom work.

The goals of this book are two-fold: (1) to help Chinese Christians and church leaders in US Chinese churches better understand the state of the missions practice of the US Chinese church, including unique advantages and areas for growth, and (2) to contribute to the fields of diaspora missiology and short-term missions research, showing how the US Chinese church helps illumine and expand these fields. These goals are achieved through examining and analyzing what kind of role, if any, diaspora plays in global outreach today, as well as interacting with the theories of global diaspora and diaspora missiology. The study focuses particularly on Chinese churches in diaspora in the USA using both quantitative research (survey methodology) and qualitative research (formal interviews). Through these methods, general information and the mission activities of US Chinese churches are reported and interpreted. Hence, this study enables short-term missions scholars and practitioners to understand the distinction between the STM practice of US Chinese churches and American churches, while also helping Chinese Christians in the USA learn how their mission practice fits in with the larger picture of diaspora mission in a globalized world.

Scope and Delimitation

This study includes the mission activities which are common in US Chinese churches; for example, mission conferences, short-term missions and supporting overseas mission work. It is focused on the patterns of diaspora ministry in the age of globalization and how diaspora theories and diaspora missiology can relate to them. Previous studies on US megachurches and US Korean churches are also used to make comparisons and to support the central argument.

The study does not cover other frequently discussed issues of short-term mission, such as whether short-term mission leads to long-term spiritual transformation of the participants, whether short-term missions bring more long-term missionaries, the social engagement of short-term mission participants, the response and feedback from the local people who receive short-term mission teams, the expenses of short-term mission trips and how they are paid, and issues of partnership in short-term mission.

CHAPTER 2

Diaspora and Mission in the Age of Globalization

It is a commonly held notion among Chinese Christians that Chinese churches tend to invest more in ministries to their own kinsmen and collaborate with their kinsmen in missions. But is this true, and if so, why? In order to understand the phenomena of US diaspora Chinese mission, we must place it in the context of the realities of diaspora, globalization, and mission generally as well as with the Chinese specifically. The study of Chinese congregations in the USA and their mission practices therefore requires the convergence of various fields. Four specific areas will be covered in this chapter. First, we review the theories of diaspora and globalization. Second, we examine Chinese diaspora – how it is formed, relations with the homeland, etc. – through a survey of Chinese immigrant communities from a historical and sociological perspective. Third, the idea of "diaspora missiology" is introduced, as well as its application in the Chinese context. Fourth, we review prior studies on the short-term mission movement in North America, including some critiques of the movement.

Theories of Globalization and Diaspora

Globalization

The term "globalization" was first used in the 1980s by sociologist Roland Robertson, and it was later adopted by other scholars in the studies of various international flows – "human, economic, and financial, but especially informational and cultural ones."[1] Globalization has been a frequently discussed topic in the fields of social science in the past two decades. Generally speaking, globalization can be observed in these dimensions: economic, political, cultural, ecological and in communication.[2] Historical sociologist Robert J. Holton summaries different views on globalization and gives a definition of globalization as:

1) The intensified movement of goods, money, technology, information, people, ideas and cultural practices across political and cultural boundaries. Such movements combine cause and effect. They implicate the interests and activities of merchants and bankers, migrants and religious leaders, media representatives and activists.

2) The interdependence of social process across the globe, such that all social activity is profoundly interconnected rather than separated off into different national and cultural spaces. Once again interdependence arises out of human activity and involves particular agents, whether global entrepreneurs or regulators, medical professionals or lawyers, social movement activists or world musicians. It involves formally organized undertaking as well as those embodied in networks and looser forms of cooperation and conflict.

3) Consciousness of and identification with the world as a single place, as in forms cosmopolitanism, religion or earth-focused environmentalism. This approach, pioneered by Roland Robertson (1995) embraces global imaginings and is thus also centrally concerned with initiative and undertaking. Cosmopolitanism, moreover, is not an exclusively Western orientation (Cheah and Robbins 1998, Holton 2002) and this alerts us to the multicultural roots of global consciousness.[3]

---

1. Stéphane Dufoix, *Diasporas* (Berkeley, CA: University of California Press, 2008), 31.

2. A. C. Besley, "Hybridized and Globalized: Youth Cultures in the Postmodern Era," *The Review of Education, Pedagogy, and Cultural Studies* 25 (2003): 162.

3. Robert J. Holton, *Making Globalization* (New York: Palgrave Macmillan, 2005), 14–15.

Holton's definition draws attention to the international migration and activities of humans beyond just materials and ideas, though he does not treat it as a major theme of globalization.

Sociologist Saskia Sassen believes globalization includes two sets of dynamics: (1) the formation of explicitly global institutions and processes, the WTO for example, and (2) the processes that do not necessarily scale at the global level but are still part of globalization, for example, certain national fiscal policy.[4] She uses traditional sociological objects such as social structure, social practices and institutions to study global process; most of her arguments are built upon empirical references to real issues such as historical events (e.g. the collapse of Soviet Union), world economy, policies or treaties (e.g. NAFTA) and certain global cities. In global cities (i.e. New York, London, Tokyo, Paris, Frankfurt, Zürich, Los Angeles, Toronto, Sydney, Hong Kong, Shanghai, etc.), this kind of global process leads to "transnational economics and political opening" and thus brings in "transnational actors."[5] She further identifies three major migration links to connect the sending and receiving countries: (1) links brought about by economic globalization (e.g. workers from low-wage countries to work for firms in highly developed countries), (2) links and an ethnic network developed to recruit workers (e.g. ethnic Polish workers in Germany one century ago), and (3) the legal and illegal organized export of workers (e.g. the Philippines' current policy of workers export, and women trafficking).[6]

Many raise the question of whether globalization equals westernization or Americanization. This perspective on globalization would observe the success of certain global brands such as Starbucks, McDonalds, Apple, Hollywood movies, Western TV shows and celebrity singers, movie stars and athletes. These are all images that appear on a regular basis in the mainstream media. However, some scholars point out that "globalization does not simply position Asian cultures as naïve victims of rapacious Western multinationals."[7] Holton also believes that globalization "is not

---

4. Saskia Sassen, *A Sociology of Globalization* (New York: W. W. Norton & Company, 2007), 5–6.

5. Sassen, *A Sociology of Globalization*, 128.

6. Ibid., 141–142.

7. Besley, "Hybridized and Globalized," 169.

an exclusively Western orientation."[8] The popularity of Japanese animé, Japanese video games and Korean dramas in Asia is a good example. Scholars also find one of the reasons for the success of Japanese and Korean popular culture is that they both present a good mixture of Western and Asian culture.[9] As Kjeldgaard and Askegaard quote from Marketing News (2002): "Last year I was in 17 countries, and it's pretty difficult to find anything that is different, other than language, among a teenager in Japan, a teenager in the UK and a teenager in China."[10] "Hybridity," as well as terms such as "tribes," "neo-tribes," lifestyles," etc., are often used by postmodern writers to portray youth subcultures.[11] Multinational corporations' marketing strategies play an important role in this hybridizing process. They target specific age and interest groups and label them through commercials and media.[12] In this way, young people receive the global pop culture in their own local context and form their identity.[13] In addition, the term "glocalization" is used in contrast to globalization, which implies that globalization is always localized in a certain local context while some local culture is globalized.[14] Besley's comment describes this complexity well:

---

8. Holton, *Making Globalization*, 15.

9. For example, Lam comments that "in many of these [Japanese] books, different types of Westernized or Americanized images appear in parts of the texts" (Wan Shun Eva Lam, "Border Discourses and Identities in Transnational Youth Culture," in *What They Don't Learn in School: Literacy in the Lives of Urban Youth*, ed. Jabari Mahiri, [New York: Peter Lang, 2004], 10), and Korean pop culture also "skillfully blends Western and Asian values to create its own" (Doobo Shim, "Hybridity and the Rise of Korean Popular Culture in Asia," *Media, Culture & Society* 28, no. 1 [2006]: 40). In other words, Japanese and Korean pop culture effectively present a kind of hybridity.

10. Dannie Kjeldgaard and Søren Askegaard, "The Glocalization of Youth Culture: The Global Youth Segment as Structures of Common Difference," *Journal of Consumer Research* 33, no. 2 (2006): 231.

11. Anoop Nayak, *Race, Place and Globalization: Youth Cultures in a Changing World* (Oxford: Berg, 2003), 19.

12. Besley, "Hybridized and Globalized"; Kjeldgaard and Askegaard, "The Glocalization of Youth Culture."

13. Besley comments, "Youth will often blend different cultural styles through an active, creative, hybridizing process that produces a new product from preformed materials, but generally does not invent new cultural and aesthetic resources per se" (Besley, "Hybridized and Globalized," 172).

14. Kjeldgaard and Askegaard, "The Glocalization of Youth Culture."

"Globalization can diminish yet may also intensify political domination, and lead to both homogeneity as well as pluralized cultural identities."[15]

Is there any cause-effect relation between globalization and global diaspora? Robin Cohen lists five aspects of globalization in his book *Global Diaspora*: (1) a world economy, (2) forms of international migration, (3) the development of "global cities," (4) the creation of cosmopolitan and local cultures, and (5) a deterritorialization of social identity.[16] In this sense, globalization can be present in the form of international firms and workers, products, knowledge, fashions which prevail across the border, interdependence on international politics and economics, etc. With a focus on international human migration, Cohen concludes in his study that, "globalization and diasporization are separate phenomena with no necessary causal connections, but they 'go together' extraordinarily well."[17]

This research mainly focuses on Chinese diaspora, their mission activities and transnational ties. These concern the movement of human beings, and thus Saskia Sassen's ideas of transnational actors and ethnic networks of globalization are most helpful here. From previous studies we see the complexity of the relations among globalization, human migration and diaspora. Although diaspora and globalization are related to each other, we treat them as two different phenomena. One of the most apparent reasons is that diaspora predates globalization, having existed for thousands of years (e.g. the Jewish diaspora). The history and terminology of diaspora will be discussed in the next section.

Diaspora

Scholars of different disciplines have been defining and refining the term "diaspora" over the past three decades. The term "diaspora" has had a broad usage since the 1980s by sociologists, political scientists, anthropologists, economists, and more recently, missiologists. Certainly diaspora is a relatively new term in social science, and recently its meaning has broadened. French sociologist Stéphane Dufoix even uses "the ambiguities of a cliché"

---

15. Besley, "Hybridized and Globalized," 162.

16. Robin Cohen, *Global Diasporas: An Introduction* (Seattle: University of Washington Press, 1997).

17. Cohen, *Global Diasporas*, 175.

to describe its broad usage and suggests that "'Diaspora' now means 'ethnic community separated by state borders' or 'transnational community'."[18] Dufoix further explains that the extension of its usage may be due to "the influences of theories of globalization and postmodernism since the 1980s."[19]

The word "diaspora" is the direct phonetic transcription from the Greek noun *diaspora*. Its verb of the same root, *diaspero*, is a combination of the Greek verb *speiro* (to sow) and the preposition *dia* (over). Its infinitive, *diaspeirein*, originally refers to an agricultural process of "the fruitful scattering away of seeds,"[20] and thus it carries the meaning of "to scatter over." The earliest usage of the term *diaspora* can be traced back further to the fifth century BC by Thucydides, referring to the dispersal of Aeginetans.[21] The earliest biblical usage of this term occurs in the Greek translation of Deuteronomy 28:25 in the Septuagint (LXX) of the third century BC, referring to the scattered Jews: "Thou shalt be a dispersion (*en diaspora*) in all kingdoms of the earth."[22] Later, in Deuteronomy 28:58–68 the word continues to convey the idea of diaspora as "a forcible dispersion."[23] In the New Testament, this Greek word is repeatedly used to describe the situation of Jews as a dispersed community in the first century under the rule of Roman Empire (John 7:35; 1 Pet 1:1; Jas 1:1). When John, James and Peter used the term *diaspora* they did not modify it with the word "Jews" (*Ioudaios*), which may imply that the term *diaspora* in that era was particularly used for diaspora Jews rather than all ethnicities.

From these early usages, we see the word diaspora has a close relationship with Jewish history. However, this term was not used frequently until the nineteenth century, and its early usages were either referring to the Jews who were scattered after the Exile or Christian communities such as the Moravians. The early study of diaspora can be traced to the late nineteenth

---

18. Dufoix, *Diasporas*, 30.

19. Ibid.

20. Khachig Tölölyan, "Rethinking Diaspora(s): Stateless Power in the Transnational Moment," *Diaspora* 6, no.1 (1996): 10.

21. Gabriel Sheffer, *Diaspora Politics: At Home Abroad* (Cambridge, UK: Cambridge University Press, 2003), 9; Dufoix, *Diasporas*, 4.

22. Sheffer, *Diaspora Politics*, 9 (Scripture translation from Brenton's English Septuagint, 1851).

23. Cohen, *Global Diasporas*, 1.

century.[24] The term became more widely assimilated into English by the mid-twentieth century when there was a trend in the study of ancient Jewish diaspora.[25] This term was primarily religious until the 1950s, when sociologists attempted to extend its usage to a general concept.[26] Yet diaspora was not listed in the 1968 edition of the Encyclopedia of Social Sciences.[27] In the 1980s, sociologists and political scientists started to define this term. In 1991, the sociology journal *Diaspora* was issued, which provided a forum for more dialogue and study of this topic. Different definitions will be discussed below.

In 1986, political scientist Gabriel Sheffer put forward a definition of diaspora in his article, *A New Field of Study: Modern Diasporas in International Politics*: "Modern diasporas are ethnic minority groups of migrant origins residing and acting in host countries but maintaining strong sentimental and mental links with their countries of origin – their homeland."[28] In 2003, he introduced a term "ethnonational diaspora" and adjusted the former definition in his book *Diaspora Politics* to:

> An ethnonational diaspora is a social-political formation, created as a result of either voluntary or forced migration, whose members regard themselves as of the same ethnonational origin and who permanently reside as minorities in one or several host countries. Members of such entities maintain regular or occasional contacts with what they regard as their homelands and with individuals and groups of the same background residing in other host countries. Based on aggregate decisions to settle permanently in host countries, but to maintain a common identity, diasporans identify as such, showing solidarity with their group and their entire nation, and they organize and are active in the cultural, social, economic, and political

---

24. L. V. Rutgers, *The Hidden Heritage of Diaspora Judaism*, 2nd ed. (Bondgenotenlaan, Belgium: Uitgeverij Peeters, 1998), 15.

25. Ibid.

26. Dufoix, *Diasporas*, 16–18.

27. Tölölyan, "Rethinking Diaspora(s)," 9.

28. Gabriel Sheffer, "A File of Study: Modern Diasporas in International Politics," in *Modern Diaspora in International Politics*, ed. Gabriel Sheffer (London: Croom Helm, 1986), 3.

spheres. Among their various activities, members of such diasporas establish trans-state networks that reflect complex relationships among the diasporas, their host countries, their homelands, and international actors.[29]

Using this definition, Sheffer focused in his book on the ethnic aspect and group identity of diaspora. He narrows down the categories of diaspora, but his definition still carries a general concept.

The first article which William Safran contributed to the journal *Diaspora* gives a multicriteria definition of diaspora. The defining characteristics of diasporas are:

> (1) they, or their ancestors, have been dispersed from a specific original "center" to two or more "peripheral," or foreign, regions; (2) they retain a collective memory, vision, or myth about their original homeland – its physical location, history, and achievements; (3) they believe that they are not – and perhaps cannot be – fully accepted by their host society and therefore feel partly alienated and insulated from it; (4) they regard their ancestral homeland as their true, ideal home and as the place to which they or their descendants would (or should) eventually return – when conditions are appropriate; (5) they believe that they should, collectively, by committed to the maintenance or restoration of their original homeland and to its safety and prosperity; and (6) they continue to relate, personally or vicariously, to that homeland in one way or another, and their ethno-communal consciousness and solidarity are importantly defined by existence of such a relationship.[30]

Safran's definition includes these elements: different locations, collective idealized homeland, alienation from host-land, hope of return, and maintaining relationship with homeland. We can see in Safran's definition a strong influence of the prototype of Jewish diaspora, as well as a much more substantial and specific definition than that of Sheffer. Tölölyan has a

---

29. Sheffer, *Diaspora Politics*, 9–10.

30. William Safran, "Diasporas in Modern Societies: Myths of Homeland and Return" *Diaspora* 1, no. 1 (1991): 83–84.

similar approach, summarizing six constitutive elements of diaspora in his article, including (1) external *coercion* causing resettlement outside of the homeland, (2) clear delimited identity in its homeland before departure, (3) active *collective* memory maintenance, (4) ethnic identity and communal boundary, (5) keeping communication with other communities of the same ethnicity, and (6) maintaining contact with the homeland.[31] Anthropologist James Clifford also quoted Safran's definition in his article "Diasporas," while he used a different approach by defining diaspora in a negative way (i.e. "diaspora is not"). According to him, diaspora is not "the norms of nation-states and indigenous, and especially autochthonous, claim by 'tribal' peoples," and it is also not merely temporarily traveling.[32]

Sociologist Robin Cohen borrows Safran's definition but makes some adjustments, emphasizing more ethnic group identity maintenance. He adds four more elements in his definition: voluntary scattering, retaining diasporic consciousness, creative transnational identity and "a common identity with co-ethnic members in other countries."[33] In this light his list of "common features of a diaspora" is as follows:

1) dispersal from an original homeland, often traumatically, to two or more foreign regions;

2) alternatively, the expansion from a homeland in search of work, in pursuit of trade or to further colonial ambitions;

3) a collective memory and myth about the homeland, including its location, history and achievements;

4) an idealization of the putative ancestral home and a collective commitment to its maintenance, restoration, safety and prosperity, even to its creation;

5) the development of a return movement that gains collective approbation;

6) the strong ethnic group consciousness sustained over time and based on a sense of distinctiveness, a common history and the belief in a common fate;

---

31. Tölölyan, "Rethinking Diaspora(s)," 12–16.

32. James Clifford, "Diasporas," *Cultural Anthropology* 9, no. 3 (1994): 307.

33. Cohen, *Global Diasporas*, 23–25.

7) a troubled relationship with host societies, suggesting a lack of acceptance at the least or the possibility that another calamity might befall the group;

8) a sense of empathy and solidarity with co-ethnic members in other countries of settlement; and

9) the possibility of a distinctive creative, enriching life in host countries with tolerance for pluralism.[34]

Like Safran, Cohen also sees Jewish diaspora as a prototype of diaspora, and he uses five different characteristics to categorize other diasporas: victim, labor, trade, imperial and cultural diaspora. In this sense, refugees of other origins or ethnicities may be called a diaspora, but the capitalized Diaspora specifically refers to Jewish diaspora. For Jews, Africans, Palestinians and Armenians "diaspora signified a collective trauma, a banishment, where one dreamed of home but lived in exile."[35]

French sociologist Stéphane Dufoix attempts to integrate theories and ideas of diaspora from different scholars in his book *Diasporas*. He uses three categories to distinguish these definitions: open definition, e.g. Sheffer; categorical definition, e.g. Safran and Cohen; and oxymoronic definition, e.g. Clifford.[36] Kim D. Butler also compares these different concepts and definitions of diaspora of scholars such as Safran, Tölölyan, Clifford and Cohen, and summarizes by saying that there are three basic features of diaspora: (1) at least two destinations for the diaspora after scattering, (2) some relationship to an actual or imagined homeland, and (3) self-awareness of the group's identity.[37]

In sum, today the definition of diaspora is still in the process of being formulated and refined. If one's definition is too broad, too many things can be called diaspora, and the term cannot reflect a specific time and space. On the other hand, if the definition is too strict, the term diaspora will become overly academic or technical and not accepted and understood by general readers, thus making it less useful in helping analyze and explain

---

34. Ibid., 26.

35. Ibid., ix.

36. Dufoix, *Diasporas*, 21–25.

37. Kim D. Butler, "Defining Diaspora, Refining a Discourse," *Diaspora* 10, no. 2 (2001): 192.

current phenomena. Thus it is necessary to adopt a definition which can best elucidate the real situation.

The present study focuses on the Chinese diaspora, and the above discussion shows that definitions of diaspora by major scholars can be used to accurately describe Chinese diaspora according to their criteria. In fact, these scholars include Chinese diaspora as one of the "classic" diasporas.[38] Safran and Cohen contain more emphasis on the shared historical experiences and the psychological complex about homeland of diaspora groups, while Sheffer addresses more of the transnational network of ethnonational diaspora groups. Since my research is dealing with contemporary mission work through Chinese diaspora, a kind of transnational activity in the Chinese Christian context, the definition with an emphasis on transnational networks will provide a more accurate description of Chinese diaspora, and therefore, for this research, I adopt the Sheffer's definition for diaspora.

Diaspora in the Globalized World

From the previous discussion we see the definitions of diaspora have changed over the past century. It used to carry a historical and religious meaning, but now refers to a new phenomenon (while the old phenomenon – Jewish diaspora – still exists). Sheffer brought up the term "modern diaspora" in his 1986 article and tried to mark the difference with "classical diaspora." Here we will further demonstrate how modern diaspora differs from classic diaspora in the Ancient Near East and Roman Empire. First, many scholars recently claim that "diasporas are made and unmade as a result of both voluntary and forced migration."[39] This is different from the traditional view of classic diasporas, which were generally the result of forced migration only. In addition, recently many scholars connect diaspora with international migrants and the concept of transnationalism in their works, sometimes viewing them as synonyms. To better understand the diaspora in the contemporary world, then, we must understand the term transnationalism and examine its relation to diaspora.

---

38. For more detailed discussion on Chinese diaspora, please see the next section "Chinese Diaspora."

39. Sheffer, *Diaspora Politics*, 114; Cohen, *Global Diasporas*; Nicholas Van Hear, *New Diasporas: The Mass Exodus, Dispersal and Regrouping of Migrant Communities* (Seattle: University of Washington Press, 1998).

The concept of transnationalism is often used by social scientists when discussing the subject of globalization. Thus to better understand diaspora in the age of globalization, we need to know the relation between transnationalism and diaspora.

According to Schiller et al., transnationalism is

> the process by which immigrants build social fields that link together their country of origin and their country of settlement. Immigrants who build such social fields are designated "transmigrants." Transmigrants develop and maintain multiple relations – familial, economic, social, organizational, religious, and political that span borders. Transmigrants take actions, make decisions, and feel concerns, and develop identities within social networks that connect them to two or more societies simultaneously.[40]

Laurence J. C. Ma recognizes the significance of transnationalism in Chinese diaspora in a 2003 article, where he focuses on the transnational activities such as trading and the globalization of "Chinese capitalism" among Chinese diasporic communities.[41] In the article, "Transnationalism and Ethnonational Diasporism," Sheffer compares transnational communities with diaspora and discusses their similarity and differences.[42] Sheffer comments that the studies on transnationalism "focused on the nature and impact of the relationships in which people at large, not necessarily migrants, had been engaged in two or more host countries."[43] These transnational groups do not "automatically organize as a diaspora" nor "create and support institutions that represent them culturally and politically," and they are not always "of the same ethnonational origin."[44] For example,

---

40. Nina Glick Schiller, Linda Basch, and Cristina Blanc-Szanton, eds. *Towards a Transnational Perspective on Migration: Race, Class, Ethnicity, and Nationalism Reconsidered* (New York: New York Academy of Sciences, 1992), 1–2.

41. J. C. Ma, "Space, Place and Transnationalism in the Chinese Diaspora," in *The Chinese Diaspora: Space, Place, Mobility, and Identity*, ed. J. C. Ma and Carolyn Cartier (Lanham, MD: Roman & Littlefield, 2003), 24.

42. Gabriel Sheffer, "Transnationalism and Ethnonational Diasporism," *Diaspora* 15, no. 1 (2006).

43. Ibid., 123.

44. Ibid., 124.

dispersed Muslims or overseas Latinos, sharing the same religion and/or languages with others in their group, can be transnational communities but have multiple ethnicities. According to Sheffer, they cannot be called diaspora, but if classified by ethnonational groups, they can be "Mexican" or "Colombian" diaspora, and "Somali" or "Pakistani" diaspora.[45] He points out one of the main differences between transnational migrants and ethnonational diaspora is that transnational migrants "tend either to assimilate or to integrate fully into their host societies" and "their memories of their historical and more recent ancestors or of their 'original homelands' do not remain significant for their continued existence as coherent entities."[46]

On the other hand, Holton understands transnationalism as an "umbrella concept, in which multiple phenomena, both material and symbolic, are involved, that stretch or range in some way beyond the national," when compared with the concept of globalization.[47] He discovers in many ways transnationalism and globalization can link to the same ideas, yet transnationalism is a simpler process than globalization in the way that transnationalism only requires the process of being cross-border and more than one national identity, while globalization "involves more striking claims to span the globe."[48] Thus he may be right when he says that "some of the networks labelled as global might more helpfully be labelled transnational."[49]

To sum up, it may be more accurate to use "transnational/transnationalism" rather than "global/globalization" when studying diasporas. Although transnationalism is a broader term than diaspora, many characteristics and activities of diaspora can be identified as transnational. Now that we have clarified these widely used concepts and terms, we move forward to the Chinese diaspora, especially focusing on Chinese immigrants in the United States.

---

45. Ibid., 130.
46. Ibid., 127–128.
47. Robert Holton, *Global Networks* (New York: Palgrave Macmillan, 2008), 44.
48. Ibid., 44.
49. Ibid., 45.

Chinese Diaspora

"Chinese" is an umbrella term in English which includes various meanings in the Chinese language. Chinese can refer to (1) national Chinese, Zhōngguórén,[50] those who hold citizenship of People's Republic of China, (2) overseas Chinese migrants or immigrants, Huáqiáo,[51] (3) ethnic Chinese who are the descendants of Chinese immigrants, Huáyì,[52] or (4) a broad sense, Huárén, which includes all three of the above.[53] Another term (5) overseas Chinese, Haiwai Huárén[54] – which includes (2) Chinese migrants or immigrants Huáqiáo, and (3) their descendants Huáyì – is more often used when discussing Chinese diaspora. The term Chinese diaspora is closest to the meaning of overseas Chinese Haiwai Huárén; however, based on a more strict definition of diaspora, migrants are not considered as diaspora. Here in this research the term "Chinese" refers to Huárén, and the term "overseas Chinese" includes both diaspora Chinese and Chinese migrants.

Regarding ethnicity,[55] there are five major Chinese ethnic groups (Han, Manchu, Mongol, Hui and Tibetan). Han Chinese is the majority (91.3%), and among the diaspora Han Chinese there is a cluster of seventeen Han Chinese language groups. They form the largest ethnic group in

---

50. 中國人 Zhōngguórén
51. 華僑 Huáqiáo
52. 華裔 Huáyì
53. 華人 Huárén
54. 海外華人 Haiwai Huárén
55. In Western languages there are terms such as *Volk, ethnos,* race, tribe and nation. Chinese people originally used the term "*minzu*" (民族) to convey this idea, which was first used as early as the sixth century in the *Book of Southern Chi.* This term literally means "people group" or "tribe" and is close to the idea of ethnicity in English, *ethnos* in Greek or *Volk* in German. As for the term "race" and "nation," it is a more Western idea. Through a long history of thousands of years, the concept of ethnicity of Chinese people is distinct from the West, and even the concept of Chinese people is very vague. Another phrase, "Chinese ethnic group" (*zhong hua min zu*), also translated "Chinese nation," is a modern idea, first used in the early twentieth century by the scholar and politician Liang Chi-Chao (1873–1929) to include all the ethnic groups, e.g. Han, Manchu, Mongol, Hui and Tibetan, etc., in China (Xisuo Li, (李喜所). 梁啟超是提出"中華民族"稱謂的第一人. 人民網, 2006, http://theory.people.com.cn/BIG5/49157/49163/4089792.html [accessed 22 February 2014], 2006). This term, however, is confusing, since there is no such usage in other countries, like American ethnic group or Nigerian ethnic group. In fact, Manchu, Mongol, Hui, Tibetan and other ethnic groups were even not considered as Chinese before the twentieth century.

the world, numbering about 1.2 billion.[56] This research uses census and survey data in which respondents identified themselves as Chinese in the questionnaires. In censuses and surveys, the options of ethnicity are the umbrella term "Chinese" or "other Asian." From previously mentioned data we know those who answered "Chinese" are most likely Han (91.3%). Self-identification is a major part of ethnicity,[57] and thus even though some respondents might be Manchu, Mongol, Hui or other ethnic groups – they self-identify as "Chinese" in a survey and not "other Asian" – it is legitimate to include them in research on Chinese diaspora.

According to the data updated in 2010, there are 71 million overseas ethnic Chinese (i.e. Chinese immigrants and their descendants around the world) (CCCOWE 2011).[58] This number includes those who live in Taiwan and hold the citizenship of Republic of China, Taiwan (23 million), and those who live in Hong Kong and Macao (7.6 million). Geographically, most of the Chinese diaspora dwell in Asia, and especially in Southeast Asia: the Philippines, Malaysia, Singapore, Indonesia, Thailand, Vietnam, and Myanmar, with a total of about 61 million, which is about 86 percent of the total overseas Chinese population. Second is North America, which contributes 5.5 million (with 4 million in the USA) and 7.7 percent of the total. Third is Latin America where there are about 1.8 million ethnic Chinese. Europe also has 1.3 million, and Oceania and Africa have 0.9 million and 0.7 million, respectively (CCCOWE 2011).

---

56. Patrick Johnstone and Jason Mandryk, *Operation World* (Colorado Springs, CO: Global Mapping International, 2001), 159.

57. George De Vos, *Ethnic Identity: Creation, Conflict and Accommodation* (Walnut Creek, CA: Altamira, 1995), 25; Eghosa Osaghae, "On the Concept of the Ethnic Group in Africa: A Nigeria Case," *Plural Societies* 16, no. 2 (1986): 166.

58. See www.cccowe.org for the sources of the Overseas Chinese population data of CCCOWE.

Region	Overseas Chinese population	Percent
Asia	60,765,000	85.1%
North America	5,510,000 (4,178,000 in USA)	7.7%
Latin America	1,806,150	2.5%
Europe	1,368,300	1.9%
Oceania	954,050	1.3%
Africa	723,000	1.0%
Middle East	259,200	0.4%
Total	**71,385,700**	**100.0%**

Table 2.1. Overseas Chinese Population (data from CCCOWE 2011)

Classic Chinese Diaspora

The classic Chinese diaspora is categorized as "trade diaspora" according to Cohen's definition.[59] The trading and business activities between China, South Asia and Southeast Asia can be traced to the Tang dynasty (AD 618–907), but it was not as significant as that of late Song dynasty (AD 980–1276).[60] Later during the Ming dynasty (AD 1368–1644), the "heyday of ancient China's maritime enterprise," Chinese traders started to build up their community around the South and the East China Sea, for instance, with settlements in Manila in the 1570s and Nagasaki after 1600.[61] These overseas Chinese communities continue to grow in the Philippines, Japan, Java, Malaysia, Thailand, etc. During the second half of the nineteenth century a large number of migration laborers (*coolie*) flowed out of China, mainly heading to North America and Austria as miners and rail builders. These early migrant workers also built up overseas Chinese communities such as Chinatown in San Francisco around the 1840s. A significant diaspora as exile happened in the seventeenth century after the Ming dynasty was overturned by the Qing dynasty (AD 1644–1912). Since the ethnicity of Qing's royal house was not Han Chinese, a group of Han Chinese loyal

---

59. Cohen, *Global Diasporas.*
60. Wang, *The Chinese Overseas*, 23.
61. Ibid., 87–97.

to the Ming dynasty fled to Taiwan and built up a short dynasty there (AD 1661–1683) to prepare for a future uprising against the Qing dynasty.[62]

These early overseas Chinese in Southeast Asia fit very well within the theories and definitions of diaspora discussed above (Sheffer, Amersfoort and Van Hear). They had their own boundary-maintaining institutions; some for education, teaching their children the Chinese language and Confucian values;[63] some ethnic (e.g. ancestry shrine or memorial hall); and some religious (e.g. temples of Buddhism or folk religion).[64] Under these institutions overseas Chinese practiced communal rituals in their daily life, and thus their Chinese identity was reinforced.[65] In addition, the British colonial policy in Southeast Asia allowed various ethnic groups to maintain their cultural practices, and later national government provided a bilingual education system, and thus Chinese diaspora in Southeast Asia usually mastered local languages and Chinese dialects.[66] Besides, being active traders they generally were wealthy and had high socioeconomic status.[67] Yet many scholars (Cohen, Ma, Fan, Pan, etc.) point out the fact that historically traditional diaspora Chinese had suffered from discrimination of their host countries, and it does not matter whether they were well off economically in South-East Asia or laborers (*coolie*) in North America. They also had a close relationship with the homeland, cared about and were even involved in the political activities of their homeland. One of the most significant examples is revolution movements during the late Qing dynasty. When Dr Sun Yat-Sen (1866–1925), the founder of Republic of China (1911–present) started to advocate revolution in the late nineteenth

---

62. See for example, Lynn Pan, ed. *The Encyclopedia of the Chinese Overseas*. 2nd ed. (Singapore: Editions Didier Millet, 2006), 48–49.

63. Wang, *The Chinese Overseas*, 213.

64. Adam McKeown, "Ethnographies of Chinese Transnationalism," *Diaspora* 10, no. 3 (2001): 352.

65. Chee-Kiong Tong and Kwok-bun Chan, "One Face, Many Masks: The Singularity and Plurality Chinese Identity," *Diaspora* 10, no. 3 (2001): 372.

66. Ibid., 375–377.

67. Wang, *The Chinese Overseas*, 125–127.

century, a good amount of revolutionaries and the majority of donors and supporters were overseas Chinese.[68]

Modern Chinese Diaspora

After the People's Republic of China was established in 1949, the dynamic of Chinese diaspora and the homeland changed. Emigrants were suspected by the communist government of "having ties to foreign imperialism."[69] Millions of Chinese fled to Hong Kang and Taiwan around late 1940s and early 1950s, and later some of them re-migrated to other countries beyond Hong Kong and Taiwan. About the same period of time many descendants of early immigrants in Southeast Asia also re-migrated to other countries (e.g. Western Europe), because the unfriendly atmosphere in Southeast Asia against Communist China generated suspicion against these Chinese descendants (i.e. suspicion that the Chinese immigrants might be allied with communists in their homeland).[70] As Cohen comments, "After the Chinese Revolution in 1949, the ideological rift between the People's Republic and the diaspora was often too great to be bridged and practical arrangements for continuing and oscillating system of migration became increasingly troublesome."[71]

The number of earlier Chinese immigrants in the United States did not have significant growth due to the immigration law, the "1882 Chinese Exclusion Act."[72] A new wave of Chinese diaspora has taken place in North America since the 1960s. After the passage of the Immigration Act of 1965, large scale Chinese immigration started to occur in the USA. The situation was similar in Canada after Canada changed its immigration policy in 1967. Before the late 1980s most of Chinese immigrants were from Hong Kong and Taiwan, and some from Southeast Asia, who were those Chinese descendants who "re-migrated." Flow from mainland China has increased

---

68. F. E. Jandt, *An Introduction to Intercultural Communication: Identities in a Global Community*, 6th ed. (Thousand Oaks, CA: Sage, 2007), 85; see also Wang, *The Chinese Overseas*.

69. Dufoix, *Diasporas*, 49.

70. Wang, *The Chinese Overseas*, 9, 140.

71. Cohen, *Global Diasporas*, 89.

72. C. Cindy Fan, "Chinese Americans: Immigration, Settlement, and Social Geography," in *The Chinese Diaspora: Space, Place, Mobility, and Identity*, ed. J. C. Ma and Carolyn Cartier (Lanham, MD: Roman & Littlefield, 2003), 265.

more and more since the "Reform and Opening Up" of the People's Republic of China (PRC). During the 1980s and 1990s the number of PRC students and scholars grew very fast and became the largest international group in colleges.[73] Today, among all Asian groups in the USA, the Chinese is the largest. According to the census data of 2010, Chinese make up 23 percent of the Asian population in the USA; the second is Asian Indian, which is 19 percent, and the third is Filipino, which is 17 percent.[74] Fan reports that "the majority of Chinese Americans are foreign born," and the foreign born accounted for 76.6 percent and 70.7 percent of Chinese in the US in 1980 and 1990, respectively.[75]

In sum, diaspora is not just any ethnic immigration group. Distinguishing diaspora from migration, immigration and ethnic groups can help us to analyze the formation of diaspora and their identity maintenance. In order to understand the formation of diaspora, we should consider structural elements such as political economy and boundary-maintaining institutions, in addition to the discrimination from the mainstream of the host countries, e.g. exclusive immigration laws. We see this clearly in the case of both the Jewish diaspora and Chinese diaspora.

Diaspora Missiology

The term "diaspora missiology" has been used since 2004,[76] and scholars such as Enoch Wan, Sadiri Joy Tira, and Luis Patoja have written on the topic since then. However, the word "diaspora" as used by them refers to "the phenomenon of 'dispersion' or movement of any ethnic group,"[77] which carries somewhat different meanings from the meanings discussed by the sociologists and political scientists in previous sections. What Wan and his colleagues mean as "diaspora" actually includes both diaspora and ethnic migrants such as migrant workers. Sheffer suggests that the ethnic

---

73. Wang and Yang, "Evangelical and Ethnic," 181.

74. See http://www.census.gov/prod/cen2010/briefs/c2010br-11.pdf, p. 16 (accessed 27 March 2014).

75. Fan, "Chinese Americans," 262.

76. Wan, *Diaspora Missiology*, 103.

77. Luis Pantoja Jr, Sadiri Joy Tira, and Enoch Wan, eds. *Scattered: The Filipino Global Presence* (Manila, Philippines: LifeChange, 2004).

diasporas are made of "voluntary and forced international migrations of ethnic groups" through "their permanent settlement," e.g. refugees and immigrants.[78] Thus in this sense, the time period of stay and the decision of permanent stay of the migrants in the host countries is a key to determine whether they are diaspora or migrants.[79] Further, Sheffer adjusts Van Hear's theory (1998) and understands migration order as "migrants into incipient diasporas," "incipient into mature diasporas," and "diasporas into migrants and returnees."[80]

In other words, diaspora missiologists generally hold a broad view of the concept of diaspora. They define migrant workers and international students as diaspora, while sociologists and political scientists (e.g. Cohen, Safran, Sheffer and Van Hear) do not.

Some transnational people groups defined as "diaspora" (e.g. Filipinos and Koreans) by diaspora missiologists are usually defined as migrants or incipient diaspora by sociologists or political scientists. For example, Sheffer sees three categories of diasporas: (1) the main historical diasporas, formed in antiquity or during the Middle Ages (e.g. Chinese, Gypsy, Jewish and Armenian diaspora), (2) modern diasporas, created since the middle of seventeenth century (e.g. Italian and Irish) and (3) incipient diasporas (e.g. Korean, Thai, and Russian in the former Soviet Union).[81] Thus, when we are reading among different disciplines, we must carefully

---

78. Sheffer, *Diaspora Politics*, 16; Traditionally economists use push-pull factors to explain international migrations: (1) unfavorable conditions in one place, and (2) favorable conditions outside and beyond the original location (Tereso C. Casino, "Why People Move? A Prolegomenon to Diaspora Missiology," in *Korean Diaspora and Christian Mission*, ed. S. Hun Kim and Wonsuk Ma [Eugene, OR: Wipf and Stock, 2011], 36). Currently, cross-border migrations include businessmen, international students, tourists, guest workers, and asylum-seekers, etc. The difficulty is that all these groups above may have the potential to be permanent residents in the host countries, and the traditional migration theory cannot explain why they choose to stay.

79. How do migrants become diaspora? Nicolas Van Hear uses the term "the making of diaspora" to introduce this concept. He follows Massey and other scholars' economic theory of migration and develops the theory of "migration order" with six components: (1) individual decision-making and motivation, (2) household decision-making and strategies, (3) disparities between places of origin and destination, (4) the state of development of migrant networks and institutions, (5) the migration regime, and (6) macro-political economy (Van Hear, *New Diasporas*, 14–16). He looks carefully at the whole spectrum of factors, from individual to global trends, which shape international migration order.

80. Sheffer, *Diaspora Politics*, 131–145.

81. Ibid., 23.

attend to the definitions of these terms and discern if they mean the same thing. Furthermore, in conducting research, we need to carefully define these terms for the people group of our research topic. In my study, since I focus on Chinese churches in the USA, and many attendees of the Chinese church are immigrants, there is no problem in defining this group of people as diaspora according to Sheffer or other scholars like Cohen and Safran.

Diaspora Missiology in Chinese Context

Chinese-speaking churches around the world have been more aware and more actively involved in mission activities in the last two decades. Due to political issues, the major mission activities are undertaken by Chinese diaspora – such as ethnic Chinese in Hong Kong, North America, and Southeast Asia – rather than those in mainland China. The state-sanctioned churches are controlled by the PRC government through the "Three-Self Patriotic Movement Committee" of the Protestant Churches, which "functions as an extension" of the Religious Affair Bureau.[82] There is no open door for international/Western mission organizations to establish a branch in mainland China. A good example is found in an article on short-term mission, where Wan and Hartt interview four ethnic Chinese leaders of the branches of international mission organizations and all of them are Chinese diaspora in Hong Kong, Singapore, Philippines and some other country.[83]

As Enoch Wan points out in his research, "The recent population growth of diaspora Chinese provides unprecedented mission opportunities and at the same time poses a critical challenge in Christian mission – 'making disciples' as mandated in the Great Commission."[84] In 1976, as a response to the 1974 International Congress on World Evangelism in Lausanne, some seventy overseas Chinese church leaders started the first Chinese Congress on World Evangelization in Hong Kong, and later the Chinese Coordination Centre of World Evangelism (CCCOWE) was established,

---

82. For more details on how PRC regulates religions, c.f. Religion in China: Survival and Revival under Communist Rule (Yang, *Religion in China*, 77).

83. Enoch Wan and Geoffrey Hartt, "Complementary Aspects of Short-Term Missions and Long-Term Missions: Case Studies for a Win-Win Situation," in *Effective Engagement in Short-Term Missions: Doing It Right!*, ed. Robert Priest (Pasadena, CA: William Carey Library, 2008).

84. Wan, *The Chinese Diaspora*, 37.

which started the CCCOWE movement (CCCOWE 2013). According to their official webpage, their mission is:

- Promote public awareness of the significance of world missions among Chinese Christians and churches.
- Enhance the overall efficiency of evangelistic ministry coworkers, and their understanding of world missions.
- Facilitate collaboration among individuals, para-church organizations, and churches who have the common burden for world missions.
- Provide support to coworkers dedicated to the ministry of world missions (CCCOWE 2013).

We can see the influence of this movement by the establishment of two key Chinese mission organizations: Gospel Operation International for Chinese Christians (1995) and Great Commission Center International (1989). Remarkably, both organizations were founded in California, meaning they were founded by Chinese diaspora rather than national Chinese. Great Commission Center International functions as a publishing house and training center of Chinese Christians, sometimes organizing mission conferences for mobilization. On the other hand, Gospel Operation International for Chinese Christians is a sending agency, and its vision is, "Reaching our kinsmen, touching all nations." In other words, their missions are *first* to the Chinese diaspora in other countries. According to their mission newsletters and journals, they have more than one hundred staff workers and missionaries, and their mission fields now include Latin America, Southeast Asia, Central Asia, Europe and Africa.

The charismatic church planting movement started by the Bread of Life Christian Church in Taipei is also noteworthy. The mother church in Taiwan was founded in 1954, and it has planted more than 180 branches in different parts of the world among Chinese diaspora and beyond, including in Africa, Europe and America.[85] They identify their affiliation

---

85. See "Our History," Bread of Life Christian Church in Taipei (台北靈糧堂) http://www.llc.org.tw/about/history.php (accessed 27 March 2014); also see Chin T. (John) Wang, "Immigrant Churches and Their Mission: A Comparative Study of the Mission Practices among the Chinese, Hispanic, and African Immigrant Churches in New York City," PhD diss., Trinity International University, 2013, 130.

system as "the Bread of Life family." This affiliation system is also a good example of diaspora mission in the Chinese context.

In the article, "The CCCOWE Movement and World Evangelization," Thomas Wang explains the spiritual significance of the Chinese church in diaspora in this way:

> God has placed Chinese churches in many countries around the world, not only that fellow overseas Chinese may come to Christ, but people in the host countries too may be led to a saving knowledge of our Lord – just like Joseph helped both the Egyptians and his own kinsmen. The mutual responsibility of the overseas Chinese and the people in their host countries to serve God is something the overseas Chinese Church today must strive to assume and be committed to. (CCCOWE 1989)

This kind of missiology is a good representation of the more recent theories of diaspora missiology: "mission to diaspora, mission through diaspora and mission by/beyond diaspora."[86] The present study tests how prevalent or dominating this "progressional" way of doing mission is in US Chinese churches today.

Short-Term Mission as Diaspora Collaboration

When reading the book of Acts carefully, we find that all mission work in which the apostles had been involved were actually short-term missions. However, their short-term missions were very different from those most North Americans participate in today, which are cross-cultural.[87] Instead, they were more similar to the short-term missions which overseas Chinese churches are doing – missions among their kinsmen in different parts of the world. The Chinese particularism and exclusivism was similar to Jewish identity. For Chinese people, there were "either Chinese or barbarians"; for Jewish people, there were "either Jews or Gentiles." From previously mentioned literature, we can see Chinese people and Jewish people share many similar character traits, common values and beliefs in their cultures.

---

86. Wan, *Diaspora Missiology*, 138–140.

87. Robert J. Priest, Terry Dischinger, Steve Rasmussen, and C. M. Brown, "Researching the Short-Term Mission Movement," *Missiology* 34, no. 4 (2006): 433.

In general both are good at managing finances and business; both value family and education; both are scattered everywhere while maintaining their unique cultures and traditions. Therefore, it is not surprising that Chinese diaspora have many similarities with Jewish diaspora. Such a connection is noted by Carpenter: "There is just no equivalent of the overseas-born Chinese or American-born Chinese in other societies, except perhaps among the Jews."[88]

But this kind of strong ethnic identity can also be used by God for his kingdom. In the book of Acts we see how God used the Jewish diaspora in the first century to spread the gospel. Although God sent Israel into exile as a punishment for breaking the covenant at Sinai (Exod 32:1; Amos 5:25–27), he also blessed the remnant by forming them as the true people of God (Zeph 3:12–13), and this believing remnant actually became the founders of the early church and carried the task of world mission in the first century.[89] According to Acts, the apostle Paul, a diaspora Jew born in Tarsus (Acts 22:3), typically collaborated on his short-term mission trips with Jewish believers who were scattered throughout different parts of the Roman Empire. For example, Barnabas, who was a Levite born in Cyprus (Acts 4:36), accompanied Paul to Cyprus during his first mission trip (Acts 13:4). Since Barnabas was familiar with both Jewish tradition and the culture of Cyprus, he was naturally the best person to lead this short-term mission team.

Another example is that during Paul's second and third mission trip he preached in a Jewish synagogue first when he was in different cities of Greece (Acts 17:1; 17:10; 17:17). When Paul was handed over to Rome, some Jewish believers came to meet Paul and his coworkers and gave them a reception (Acts 28:15). Jewish diaspora became a touch-point or launch-pad to reach out to non-believers – including Jews and Gentiles – in the territory of the Roman Empire.

---

88. Mary Yeo Carpenter, "Familism and Ancestor Veneration: A Look at Chinese Funeral Rites," *Missiology: An International Review* 24, no. 4 (1996): 503.

89. Arthur F. Glasser with Charles E. Van Engen, Dean S. Gilliland, and Shawn B. Redford, *Announcing the Kingdom: The Story of God's Mission in the Bible* (Grand Rapids, MI: Baker, 2003), 145.

In fact, many overseas Chinese churches have been sending their own short-term mission teams, and a general perception is that most of them are sending short-term mission teams to minister to their kinsmen in China or in other countries. One purpose of this research is to verify whether this general idea is accurate or not. To better understand short-term mission, we must now focus on the short-term mission movement in the contemporary world.

Short-Term Mission in the Age of Globalization

John Stott defines mission in this way: "Mission is . . . properly a comprehensive word, embracing everything which God sends his people into the world to do. It therefore includes evangelism and social responsibility, since both are the authentic expressions of the love which longs to serve man in his need."[90] Stott's definition includes social responsibility, which fits well with short-term mission, since many short-mission trips are involved in social works.[91]

The short-term mission movement has been on the rise in the United States. Most scholars treat short-term mission as a Christian mission trip between one to two weeks, no longer than one year,[92] and this is the definition adopted in this dissertation. Short-term mission can be traced back as early as in the 1950s. At that time, mission teams took the form of music or sports evangelism teams. In the late 1950s and early 1960s, new mission organizations such as Operation Mobilization (OM) and Youth With a Mission (YWAM) started to mobilize young people to go on a short-term

---

90. John R. W. Stott, *Christian Mission in the Modern World* (Downers Grove, IL: InterVarsity, 1975), 35.

91. Charles Van Engen's definition for mission is: "the people of God, intentionally crossing barriers from Church to non-church, faith to non-faith, to proclaim by word and deed the coming of the Kingdom of God in Jesus Christ, through the Church's participation in God's mission of reconciling people to God, to themselves, to each other and to the world, and gathering them into the church through repentance and faith in Jesus Christ by the work of the Holy Spirit, with a view to the transformation of the world as a sign of the coming of the Kingdom in Jesus Christ" (see Charles Van Engen, *Mission on the Way: Issues in Mission Theology*. [Grand Rapids, MI: Baker, 1996], 26–27).

92. Recent research shows that more than 80% of short-term mission trips are between seven and thirty days, and more than one-third are between ten and fourteen days (see Priest et al., "Researching," 433).

mission trips lasting from a few weeks to a couple of years, and around the same period of time American Christian colleges also started to send summer mission trips. This movement continued to grow in the 1980s.[93] With more mission organizations founded and more local churches involved, the short-term mission movement has been well developed since then. According to the data by 2005, there are about 1.6 million adult American Christians who participate in short-term mission every year. If it costs at least $1,000 USD per person per trip, it would cost $1.6 billion USD every year on short-term missions. Further, in the same survey it also shows that 44 percent of church-goers said their church sent out short-term mission teams in the past year.[94]

Robert Wuthnow observes this phenomenon and makes a connection with globalization in his book *Boundless Faith: The Global Outreach of American Churches*. As he comments, "Globalization has tempered American Christianity. It has exposed the most devout Christians to other religions and to other ways of being Christian."[95] In this book he views the American church's overseas mission activities as "the globalization of American Christianity." Tools of transportation have improved in the past century, and thus the frequency and amount of human migration has increased significantly. Wuthnow comments, "International communication, including actually spending time in other countries, is one of the key factors driving the globalization of American Christianity."[96] The evidence is that the number of American passengers traveling to other countries has grown from ten million in 1975 to sixty million in 2000.[97]

According to Wuthnow's analysis, globalization helps the spread of American culture while the local culture is also intentionally highlighted; economically, it increases international business and reduces cost but

93. Priest, "Short-Term Mission," 84–85.

94. Robert Wuthnow and Stephen Offutt, "Transnational Religious Connections," *Sociology of Religion* 69 (2008): 218.

95. Robert Wuthnow, *Boundless Faith: The Global Outreach of American Churches*, (Berkeley, CA: University of California Press, 2009), 250.

96. Ibid., 3.

97. Wuthnow, *Boundless Faith*. See also US Department of Transportation 2000. http://www.rita.dot.gov/bts/sites/rita.dot.gov.bts/files/subject_areas/airline_information/index.html

also aggravates or ignores the poverty among the people who suffer most. "Although the demographic center of gravity is shifting to the global South, the organizational and material resources of global Christianity remain heavily concentrated in the more affluent countries of North America and Europe."[98] Since the English-speaking countries are still the most influential on the earth, the English language is still the most powerful. These superiorities of language, politics and economics make American Christianity play an essential role in this globalized world. Since globalization is an ongoing process, Christianity in the USA will continue to be affected by it and the trend of the global outreach of American churches will continue to grow strong.

The Problem of Difference and Distance

There have been many opinions of American short-term mission that have arisen in recent studies, and the questions and challenges are raised when considering short-term mission with power and economic-social issues in the "Global North-to-South" context, such as the lack of real cultural experiences,[99] the lack of good relationships with the local people,[100] the ministries being always dominated by the sending churches,[101] or the trips being designed for short-termers' spiritual benefits and not the local people.[102] As Wuthnow asks, "Are the million or so church members who go abroad on short-term mission trips helping themselves instead of serving others?"[103] Other research shows that the impact on the participants, especially young people, is limited.[104] Rick Richardson comments, "If there are

---

98. Wuthnow, *Boundless Faith*, 94.

99. Terence David Linhart, "They Were So Alive! The Spectacle Self and Youth Group Short-Term Mission Trips," *Missiology* 34, no. 4 (2006): 451–462.

100. Miriam Adeney, "When the Elephant Dances, the Mouse May Die," in *Short-Term Missions Today*, ed. Bill Berry (Pasadena, CA: Into All the World Magazine, 2003).

101. Edwin Zehner, "On the Rhetoric of the Short-Term Missions Appeals: With Some Practical Suggestions for Team Leaders," in *Effective Engagement in Short-Term Missions: Doing It Right!*, ed. Robert Priest (Pasadena, CA: William Carey Library, 2008).

102. Miriam Adeney, "Shalom Tourist: Loving Your Neighbor While Using Her," *Missiology* 34, no. 4 (2006): 463–476.

103. Wuthnow, *Boundless Faith*, 38.

104. Kurt Ver Beek, "The Impact of Short-Term Missions: A Case Study of House Construction in Honduras after Hurricane Mitch," *Missiology* 34, no. 4 (2006); and "Lessons from the Sapling: Review of Quantitative Research on Short-Term Missions," in

no follow-up structures, research suggests that there will be no behavioral changes."[105] Priest's research shows that with good culture orientation and culture-learning training, short-term mission can decrease the participants' prejudice or stereotypes toward other cultures.[106]

A study on the US megachurch shows that 59 percent of short-term mission teams are sent to Latin America and 20 percent to Africa, with the number one destination being Mexico.[107] This study also shows the strong preference to near countries as short-term mission fields. Another remarkable fact is that short-term mission has become an essential program for youth ministry in the United States. The research of the National Study of Youth and Religion shows the involvement of American youth. In 2002, 28 percent of a random sample of 3,370 adolescents had gone for a mission trip or religious service project, and in 2005 a follow-up interview to 2,604 of the same group shows that 41 percent of them had gone on a mission trip.[108]

Priest comments on social engagement of short-term mission in his article "Short-Term Mission as a New Paradigm" and chooses to use the term "linking social capital" to describe short-term mission as part of global social connectedness.[109] The flow of short-term mission presents the economic difference between sending and receiving countries since only people from affluent areas can afford trips to needy areas, but not vice versa. These North American short-term mission teams not only bring in financial resources, but also create opportunities for the local churches to connect with people of a different social status, such as "police, the mayor,

Effective Engagement in Short-Term Missions: Doing It Right!, ed. Robert Priest, (Pasadena: William Carey Library, 2008).

105. Rick Richardson, "The Impact of Urban Short-Term Projects on the Social Connections of Evangelical College Students," in *Effective Engagement in Short-Term Missions: Doing It Right!*, ed. Robert Priest (Pasadena, CA: William Carey Library, 2008).

106. Priest et al., "Researching."

107. Robert J. Priest, Douglas Wilson, and Adelle Johnson, "U.S. Megachurches and New Patterns of Global Mission," *International Bulletin of Missionary Research* 34, no. 2 (2010): 97–104.

108. Jenny Trinitapoli and Stephen Vaisey, "The Transformative Role of Religious Experience: The Case of Short-Term Missions," *Social Forces* 88, no. 1 (2009): 127.

109. Priest, "Short-Term Mission," 96.

medical personnel, gatekeepers at hospitals and jails."[110] Priest concludes that the most common benefits of linking capital are (1) shared resources, (2) open doors and enhanced credibility, and (3) strategic leverage for change and justice.[111]

To summarize these different findings on American short-term missions, most of them are reflecting the problem of "distance" and "difference"[112] (i.e. the difference of culture, language and economic-social location, and the geographic distance). The studies mentioned above show that Christians in North America tend to choose the destinations of short-term mission of shorter distance (e.g. Latin America), while there are usually significant cultural and social differences between these destinations and North America. On the contrary, US Chinese churches seem to choose mission fields of less difference, not less distance, showing transnationalism in their short-term mission practice. In other words, they do not choose to go to the places which are near, but the places where they have transnational networks. If my argument is true, (i.e. Chinese Christians tend to minister to their own kinsmen for their short-term missions), the opinions and findings above on American short-term missions may not be relevant to short-term missions carried out by Chinese churches in the United States. In chapters 4 and 5, research data is presented on US Chinese missions and short-term missions, along with further development of this argument.

In this chapter we discussed the terminology and usage of the term "diaspora," introduced the history of Chinese diaspora and how diaspora relates with mission work in the age of globalization. Next, we look at what the research data uncovers about the diaspora Chinese in the USA and their churches.

---

110. Ibid., 98.

111. Ibid., 99.

112. See for example, Wuthnow, *Boundless Faith*.

CHAPTER 3

Researching Chinese Diaspora in the USA

The mission activities of the US Chinese church are distinctive and unique. In order to understand and appreciate the distinctive quality of US Chinese mission practice, it is necessary to have a sound methodology, as well as to understand the uniquely transnational character of US Chinese Christian churches. This chapter focuses on three key areas which set the stage for an examination of the research data in the next chapter: (1) the methods of this research, (2) the uniquely transnational character of Chinese churches, and (3) a profile of Chinese churches in the USA.

Research Methods

Two primary research methods were adopted for this research, with a third supplemental method. The first part of this research is quantitative, with the instrument being a questionnaire survey. One hypothesis of this research based on observation and experiences is that "US Chinese churches invest most resources on missions to Chinese people rather than other people groups." Therefore we intended to measure how many Chinese churches are sending STM teams to Chinese areas or to minister to ethnic Chinese, and how much they invest in missions to Chinese. The second hypothesis is that "US Chinese churches undertake different activities in the mission field from other US churches for their STM trips." Some questions are designed to measure the differences, and the variables are the number of samples of overseas Chinese churches, the size of church, the frequency of short-term mission trips, the nature of work on short-term missions, the length of time for the trips, the amount of money given, the people they sent to the field and the receiving countries, etc.

The second part of this research is qualitative and was conducted through structured interviews. After gathering and analyzing the data from questionnaires, I chose six respondents to be interviewed. The interviews were conducted in Chinese. All these interviews were recorded, transcribed and translated into English. The supplemental research method is content analysis on the web pages of Chinese churches provided by different directories. One of the purposes of this content analysis was to see if these churches are still functioning. From the church web page, we also find some basic info such as the size of churches, their pastoral staff, what languages they use, and their mission activities.

Quantitative Research

There are roughly 7,200 overseas Chinese churches in Asia (excluding mainland China), 1,600 Chinese churches in North America, 300 in Europe and Oceania and 100 in Latin America (CCCOWE 2011, 8-10).[1] To narrow down this study, the research is conducted in one continent. Since I currently live and serve in the United States, and the amount of Chinese churches in the USA is remarkably large (about 1,100), I focus on Chinese churches in the USA, examining how they undertake short-term mission and how they collaborate with other Chinese diaspora. Another reason for choosing Chinese churches in the USA is to enable a direct comparison to other American churches in the USA which have been studied in previous research.

According to a recent report (2010) on the usage of technology and Internet of American churches, 90 percent of American churches use email, 69 percent have a website and 66 percent have both.[2] The first overall online survey was done through email with an electronic cover letter.

---

1. CCCOWE published their data of Oversea Chinese churches on the quarterly journal *Chinese Church Today* in 2011, where they explained that they collected this data of Chinese churches through their local branches around the world, and also used the local directories of Chinese churches produced by Chinese Christian Herald Crusades.

2. Scott Thumma, "Virtually Religious: Technology and Internet Use in American Congregations," *Faith Communities Today: American Congregations 2010*. 2010, p. 2, http://faithcommunitiestoday.org/sites/faithcommunitiestoday.org/files/Technology-Internet-Use.pdf.

I mainly used the directories provided by Ambassador for Christ, Inc. (AFC),[3] Immanuel Chinese Christian Network,[4] and Chinese Christian Herald Crusades,[5] which are overseas Chinese Christian organizations. All these directories collect the addresses and telephone numbers of Chinese churches, but not all of them include an email address. AFC's directory has more complete information, and updates monthly; the information was current up to July 2012 when I started my research. According to the directory which AFC provides, the number of Chinese churches varies from state to state. For example, in California there are about four hundred Chinese churches listed, and New York and Texas have about one hundred each, while in some states, like South Dakota and Alaska, there is no Chinese church at all.

From these directories, I collected a list of about 1,100 Chinese churches in the USA, though after searching each Chinese church on the Internet by Google search engine it appears that only about 790 of them can be confirmed that they are still active. All these 790 churches list their addresses and telephone numbers on the directories. My intent was to include those churches that have full contact information (address, phone number and email) so I had more than one way to contact them and would be able follow up with them for the survey if necessary. A judgment was made as to whether or not a church was active according to these criteria: (1) whether or not any home page or online social media page existed for the church, (2) whether addresses or contacts in different directories/pages are the same or different, and (3) whether or not any recent articles or reports mentioning this church could be found online. If one church did not have any page existing and had different addresses/contacts on different directories, and I could not find any recent article online mentioning this church, I assumed it was not active anymore. The whole process of confirming church directories took about three months. From these 790 active churches only 739 of them included email addresses on their web page. However, at that point I did not know whether or not their email addresses were valid.

---

3. http://church.oursweb.net/slocation.php?w=5&c=US&a=&t= (accessed 17 November 2012).

4. http://www.immanuel.net/OverseasChurch (accessed 17 November 2012).

5. http://cchc-herald.org/us/?page_id=49 (accessed 17 November 2012).

In January 2013, I sent out an email notice of the upcoming survey through my Trinity International University email account to these 739 Chinese churches – seventy-one of these emails bounced, and five recipients asked that they not be included in the survey. Thus I removed these churches from the list. Later, when I officially sent out the online questionnaire through SurveyMonkey in the end of January, it turned out that eleven of them had informed SurveyMonkey at some point in the past that they did not wish to receive SurveyMonkey requests, and thus SurveyMonkey itself removed them from the list. Thus the online questionnaire was sent to respondents at 652 churches. So the overall survey covered 652 Chinese churches in the USA to which I had email access, mailing addresses and telephone numbers. The time of sending the online questionnaires and receiving their response was about two months.

Bounced	Opted Out	Rejected	Real recipients	Total number of churches with email addresses
71	11	5	652	**739**

Table 3.1. Summary of Sampling

After sending out the online survey, I also sent one reminder through my TIU email account, two reminders through SurveyMonkey in February, and another one in March through SurveyMonkey. For those who started but did not complete the questionnaire, I sent one reminder in March and another one in April through SurveyMonkey. By the end of March, there were 252 churches who responded to the online survey, which is about a 38.65 percent response rate. Five more churches, which were real recipients, declined the survey through SurveyMonkey and thus opted out during these two months. Therefore, I sent out the second round of surveys with the same questionnaire by mail distribution. The mailing survey was conducted in this way: collecting mailing addresses from the names of ministers who serve in Chinese churches in USA, mailing questionnaires directly to the church leaders of non-responsive churches, which include an introduction and cover letter, return envelope, and return postcard and postage.[6] The questionnaire and introduction letter were written in both English and Chinese to ensure good communication. The mailing of the questionnaires and receiving their responses took three months. I excluded those five Chinese churches which opted out and rejected the survey.

Responded to the 1st round with answers	226
Responded to the 1st without answers	26
Opted out/rejected between two rounds	5
The 2nd round of survey sent	395
Total recipients	**652**

Table 3.2. Summary of the Two Rounds of Survey

In April 2013, I mailed out 395 hard copies of questionnaires to all the churches which had not responded. In May, I sent out another reminder through my Trinity International University email account to those who still did not respond either online or by mailing, and in July the final reminder was sent to the twenty-six churches which only answered the language preference. So in total, I sent out eight reminders, including two for those did not complete the questionnaire. By the end of August, I received eighty-eight surveys returned with answers and three more through SurveyMonkey. Thus together with the first online survey, there were 343 respondents. Then, I deleted the twenty-six online responses which only answered the language preference and did not answer any questions. Thus, the total questionnaires returned with answers were 317, a response rate of 48.61 percent (see table 3.3), a high response rate for congregational survey research.[7]

---

6. The cost of the second round survey was funded by Dr Robert Priest's research grant.

7. A previous study on survey religious research reports response rates from 17% to 30% with 10% to 19% of them responding via Internet. It also finds that clergy who serve in Asian / Pacific Islander congregations generally show a lower overall response rate (11%), with a higher percentage responding via Internet (40% of all respondents) (see Marjorie H. Royle and Destiny Shellhammer, "Potential Response Bias in Internet Use for Survey Religious Research," *Reviews of Religious Research* 49, no. 1 [2007]: 54–68).

Responded to the 1st	Responded to the 2nd	Total response	Total recipients	Response rate
226	91	317	652	48.61%

Table 3.3. Response Rate

The independent variables (i.e. church size, mission budget, mission conference frequency, number of long-term missionaries supported, mission priority, first languages of church attendees and preaching languages) and dependent variables (i.e. mission trip frequency, the impact on STM participants, short-term mission focus, short-term mission field choice and languages used in mission field) are analyzed by correlating with each other to identify the possible negative or positive correlations. Multiple correlation studies are also used when necessary as other issues arise. Data related to languages, ethnicity, receiving countries and partner churches are compared with the data of previous research on the American short-term mission movement and other ethnic American churches such as Korean American churches. All quantitative data was processed and analyzed by computer software SPSS.

Qualitative Research

According to the responses of the first online survey, I had sixteen respondents of the survey who went on STMs more than ten times, were willing to be interviewed, and left their contact information. Thus, I sent an email to these sixteen people and inquired about their availability. There were seven who responded, and six of them were available for interviews in June and July. Therefore, I had interviews with these six church leaders (five pastors and one elder) of Chinese churches. Geographically, two of them are in California, two in the Midwest, one on the East Coast and one in the South. Regarding denomination/affiliation, there is one Baptist, one with the Christian & Missionary Alliance, one Lutheran, one with Bread of Life Christian Church and two with non-denominational churches. The assumption is that since they have gone on more than ten STM trips, and they are the persons who filled out the questionnaire (and in many cases it is their church that asked them to respond to this survey), they should be the one who knows best about the mission activities in their church.

Although all of the information they provided is related to mission activity and not associated with their privacy, most of them have been involved in STM in some closed countries. For this reason, I will not identify these informants' names for security.

All interviews were conducted in Mandarin, occasionally with a little bit of English for some technical terms, and all of them are done through telephone or Skype. Each of these interviews took between 30 and 55 minutes and was conducted as structured interviews. The reason for using structured interviews is to have all the major questions fully determined ahead of time.[8] Since I already had the data from the quantitative research on hand, I needed specific information from these church leaders based on the results of the survey questionnaire.

The verbal data of the three descriptive questions from the survey was processed as qualitative data. Interview data was collected using an electronic recorder and then later transcribed, translated (from Chinese into English) and coded. Analysis and comparisons were made among the six verbal data according to the designed questions. The interview data was used to explain part of the results of the quantitative research.

Before we examine how Chinese churches in the USA carry out missions as "mission through diaspora," we need to know the key elements that have shaped the way diaspora Chinese do missions.

Homeland Relationship and Transnationalism of Chinese Diaspora

As Sheffer and Amersfoort suggest, the group identity and boundary maintenance of modern diaspora cannot be fully explained by things like linguistic ability, socioeconomic status, and residential choices, but rather more fundamental issues of psychological-cultural and shared-interest factors, homeland relationship, transnational networks, political economy and boundary-maintaining institutions. Most of the elements have existed in their society with a long history and are deeply rooted. Some of the elements have been mentioned in the previous chapter; here we will focus on

8. H. Russell Bernard, *Research Methods in Anthropology* (Lanham, MD: Altamira, 2011), 158.

the homeland relationship and transnational network, which are directly related to mission work. In the following section of this chapter we focus on these two questions. (1) What does the relation between Chinese diaspora and homeland look like now? (2) What kind of transnational networks have diaspora Chinese built up in the contemporary world?

Transnationalism in Economic Activity

When studying Chinese diaspora, we cannot neglect the relationship with their homeland – China.[9] In the aforementioned literature we see that the political and economic conditions made Chinese people move to other countries in the past several centuries. Traditionally, Chinese diaspora were viewed as traders. For example, in his book *Global Diaspora*, Cohen categorizes the traditional Chinese diaspora as "trade diaspora."[10] After the "Reform and Opening Up" of the People's Republic of China in the late 1970s and early 1980s, the economy of China has grown rapidly and now the PRC has been seen as "the twenty-first-century nation."[11] More foreigners started to learn the Chinese language, and even American high schools include Chinese in their second language curriculum. This change impacts the relation between Chinese diaspora and China.

Some of them have started to embrace the connection with China, while some have resisted.[12] In addition, globalization has impacted China economically, culturally, politically and sociologically. Today, China is the second largest economy in the world[13] and has 1.34 billion people liv-

---

9. Some may argue that Taiwanese people already developed their own identity and do not see China as their homeland. One example is that the 2010 USA census reports that 691 respondents identified them as "Other Asian" and specified "Taiwanese." Yet the USA Census Bureau still combines the data of Chinese and Taiwanese. According to diaspora theories, Taiwanese people are still part of Chinese diaspora (see Ma, "Space, Place and Transnationalism," 21).

10. Cohen, *Global Diasporas*.

11. Jandt, *Intercultural Communication*, 87, 93.

12. David Parker, "Going with the Flow?: Reflections on Recent Chinese Diaspora Studies," *Diaspora* 14, no. 2/3 (2009): 416–417.

13. Kevin Hamlin and Li Yanping, "China Overtakes Japan as the World's Second Biggest Economy," *Bloomberg News*, 16 August 2010. http://www.bloomberg.com/news/articles/2010-08-16/china-economy-passes-japan-s-in-second-quarter-capping-three-decade-rise.

ing in the country – half of them dwelling in urban areas.[14] With such a large market and business opportunities, China has been drawing investments and human resources from many different countries. As Joy Tong comments in her book *Overseas Chinese Christian Entrepreneurs in Modern China,* "particularly impressive and successful in China's economic reform have been the strategies designed to attract foreign capital."[15] According to the data of the State Statistical Bureau of China, in the first half of 2013, the ranking of the direct foreign investments in mainland China is: (1) Hong Kong (65%), (2) Japan, (3) Singapore (5.3%), (4) Taiwan (5%), (5) South Korea, (6) USA, (7) Germany, (8) Netherlands, (9) France, and (10) Thailand. The top ten countries make up about 92 percent of the total foreign investment (People's Daily 2013).[16]

It is noteworthy that the majority (more than 75%) of foreign investments are actually from the countries and areas which contain the majority of diaspora Chinese. With less language and culture barriers, it seems to make sense that Chinese diaspora have the advantage of running businesses in mainland China. Tong's study points out the significant contribution of the overseas Chinese community to China's rapid economic growth by providing the capital and expertise.[17] Laurence J. C. Ma also discovers the significance of transnational activities in the Chinese diaspora such as trading and the globalization of "Chinese capitalism" among Chinese diasporic communities.[18] Ma believes that "transnational production of Chinese diasporic capitalists has been reshaped in the last three decades into a hybrid

---

14. At the end of 2011, China counted 690.79 million urban dwellers, according to the National Bureau of Statistics. That marks an increase of 21 million over the previous year and accounts for 51.27% of the country's 1.347 billion people. During the same period, the rural population shrunk by 14.56 million to 656.56 million (Jaimes FlorCruz, "China's Urban Population Outnumbers Rural Dwellers for the First Time," 2012. http://www.cnn.com/2012/01/17/world/asia/china-urban-population-duplicate-2/index.html?hpt=wo_bn4).

15. Tong, *Entrepreneurs,* 5.

16. In 1995 before Hong Kong returned to China, the data is: (1) Hong Kong (59%), (2) Taiwan (11%), (3) the rest of OECD (8%), (4) USA, (5) Japan, (6) others, (7) Singapore, (8) rest of SE Asia (Pan, *Chinese Overseas,* 111).

17. Tong, *Entrepreneurs,* 53.

18. Ma, "Space, Place and Transnationalism," 24.

form that incorporates both traditional *guanxi* (personal relationship) networks and modern corporate culture."[19]

Transnationalism in Christian Mission

With the economic reform of China, foreign-invested enterprises in China have grown rapidly since the 1980s, which has brought in workers and visitors from all over the world.[20] At the same time, China is also the largest World B country.[21] Just as traders and businessmen fly into China from different parts of the world, Christian mission workers also find creative access to get into this religiously closed country for the large harvest. In the study on the Chinese churches in Wenzhou,[22] Nanlai Cao points out this kind of global network of Wenzhou Christianity: besides importing Bibles, books and music from overseas, "today there are overseas Christians who come to preach and teach in the local church almost every week."[23] These overseas Christians are from "Hong Kong, Taiwan, Korea, Singapore, the US, Canada, Australia, and Holland" and they "always drew large crowds" and "often received applause and flowers."[24]

Jonathan Ro studied how globalization has impacted the urban church in his dissertation by conducting congregational studies in some major churches in China,[25] and he found some examples like "the use of contemporary worship, strong Korean pastor leadership, cell-church model, pastoral leadership and highly organized ministries" and "English fellowship."[26] If diaspora Chinese have the advantage of language and culture – such as guanxi – on doing business and investments in China, do they have also

---

19. Ibid., 29.

20. Jandt, *Intercultural Communication*, 89; Shiyong Peng, *Culture and Conflict Management in Foreign-Invested Enterprises in China* (Bern: Peter Lang, 2003), 23.

21. Barrett et al., "Missiometrics."

22. Wenzhou is a city in the Southeast of China, which is well known for its capitalists and numerous active churches, the so-called "Chinese Jerusalem." For more details, please see Nanlai Cao, *Constructing China's Jerusalem: Christians, Power, and Place in Contemporary Wenzhou* (Stanford, CA: Stanford University Press, 2011).

23. Ibid., 89.

24. Ibid., 90.

25. Jonathan Ro, "Globalization's Impact on the Urban Church in China: A Multiple Case-Study of Four Churches in a Major Urban Center," PhD diss., Trinity International University, 2013.

26. Ibid., 17.

have the same advantage in Christian mission work? Do they also have significant involvement and contribution to missions in China? In fact, as Miriam Adeney mentioned at the EMS conference "Being There: Short-Term Missions and Human Need" in 2009,[27] there are four main types of STM, and Chinese people have a particular type, which is STM as Bible teaching – overseas Chinese Christians teaching or preaching the Bible to the Chinese in mainland China. This kind of short-term mission has been quite a phenomenon among Chinese churches in North America. In this research, the data shows that transnationalism exists not only in overseas Chinese economies, but also Christian missions (see the next sections). In the following sections we will focus on Chinese diaspora mission, and how overseas Chinese in the USA have developed their particular ways of doing missions.

Profile of Chinese Churches in the United States

Overview

Like other diaspora groups, Chinese immigrants in the USA also have their own boundary-maintaining institutions,[28] for example, Chinese (language) schools for teaching their children the Chinese language and Confucian values, and religious organizations and associations such as Buddhist temples, Falun Dafa associations and Chinese-speaking Christian churches. As Fenggang Yang points out in the book *Chinese Christians in America*, ethnic religious groups provide social and emotional support by "increasing social

---

27. From 30 July to 1 August 2009 hosted by Carl F. H. Henry Center at Trinity Evangelical Divinity School.

28. Amersfoort defines an immigrant population as a modern diaspora according to these: (1) First, we distinguish between immigrants who develop boundary-maintaining institutions, thereby securing intergenerational continuity, from immigrant populations assimilating into the host society. The populations with boundary-maintaining institutions are ethnic groups. (2) Ethnic groups can be classified according to their participation in central institutions of the host society, such as the labor market and the educational system. Groups that successfully participate we call established. Groups that remain, for one reason or another, confined to the lowest rungs of the social ladder form ethnic minorities. (3) Established ethnic groups that are institutionally engaged in politics with regard to their home state or home territory are modern diasporas. Ethnic groups that miss this attribute form ethnic-cultural subdivisions of the state population. (Hans van Amersfoort, "Gabriel Sheffer and the Diaspora Experience," *Diaspora: A Journal of Transnational Studies* 13, no. 2/3 [2004]: 369).

interactions among co-ethnic members and . . . providing a social space for comfort, fellowship, and a sense of belonging."[29] In addition, considering the needs of social-economic settlement as newcomers in a country, some scholars also argue that ethnic religious groups function as "bridging and bonding" social capital and facilitating "incorporation."[30] With bridging and bonding social capital, immigrants may better connect with a larger society and have more civic participation.

Lien and Carnes find Chinese "the most secular of Asian Americans," since 39 percent of them have no religious identification.[31] Their research reports that 23 percent of Chinese Americans identify themselves as Christians (including 3% as Catholic). Although this percentage is much lower than Filipino (86%), Korean (79%) and Japanese (61%) Americans,[32] it is still higher than other Chinese societies in different regions. According to the statistic data of Operation World,[33] the Christian population in Taiwan is 5.82 percent, Hong Kong 12.41 percent and mainland China 7.92 percent (estimates based on government information).[34] According to the data of CCCOWE,[35] the percentage of Christians among Chinese diaspora in Singapore and Malaysia is about 18 percent and 7.5 percent, respectively.[36] But unlike the Chinese churches in Taiwan, Hong Kong or other Chinese societies (except mainland China), today most of the Chinese churches in the USA are not missionary churches. Usually they

---

29. Fenggang Yang, *Chinese Christians in America: Conversion, Assimilation, and Adhesive Identities* (University Park, PA: The Penn State University Press, 1999), 33.

30. Michael Foley and Dean Hoge, *Religion and the New Immigrants* (New York: Oxford University Press, 2007).

31. Pei-te Lien and Tony Carnes, "The Religious Demography of Asian Boundary Crossing," in *Asian American Religions: The Making and Remaking of Border and Boundaries*, ed. Tony Carnes and Fenggang Yang (New York: New York University Press, 2004), 44.

32. Ibid.

33. Jason Mandryk, *Operation World*, 7th ed. (Colorado Springs, CO: Biblica, 2010).

34. It may be underestimated since a good amount of churches remain underground and gather secretly.

35. CCCOWE, "The Statistics Data of Overseas Chinese Population and Chinese Church," *Chinese Church Today* (今日華人教會), Hong Kong: Chinese Coordination Centre of World Evangelism, no. 281 (2011): 8–10.

36. CCCOWE published their data of Oversea Chinese Christians in the quarterly journal *Chinese Church Today* in 2011, where they also listed the sources of these data: (1) Tan, Kim Sai (2010), *Chinese Christians in Malaysia;* (2) *Census of Population* (2010) by the Singapore government. CCCOWE, p. 9.

started as Bible study groups among Chinese graduate students or a few immigrant families and then continue to develop independently of the Chinese churches.[37]

After living in the USA for more than one or two generations, Chinese Americans also adopt the American way and become non-Chinese in the eyes of "real" Chinese. Thus, they find identity and emotional support mostly in their Chinese church. As it is pointed out in the book *Chinese Christians in America*:

> For these immigrants, assimilation does not mean simply blending themselves as individuals into the American society or melting into the big American pot. Rather, they choose to congregate with fellow Chinese while studying and working or studying among non-Chinese. Living in suburbs of racially mixed neighborhoods and working or studying among non-Chinese, they find that the ethnic church provides a warm community environment for supporting immigrants and nurturing American-born youth.[38]

Yang asks, "Why do immigrants abandon their traditional religion and convert to an untraditional religion?"[39] He gives three possible reasons to discuss: to meet their physical needs, to better assimilate to the mainstream culture of American society, or to meet their ethnical needs. However, through his study he finds none of these reasons are adequate to explain the great conversions of Chinese immigrants in the USA after the 1990s; the most crucial factors are the cultural and social changes in China.[40]

Considering socioeconomic status, according to the data in 2000, 37.6 percent of Chinese immigrants born in China, 50 percent in Taiwan, and 30.1percent in Hong Kong are professional and technical. Furthermore, 13.2 percent born in China, 22.4 percent in Taiwan, and 30.6 percent in Hong Kong are executive, administrative and managerial. Additionally, 20.6 percent born in China and less than 1 percent in Taiwan and Hong

---

37. Samuel Ling, *The "Chinese Way" of Doing Things: Perspective on American-Born Chinese and the Chinese Church in North America* (San Gabriel: China Horizon, 1999), 92.

38. Yang, *Chinese Christians in America*, 191.

39. Yang, "Chinese Conversion," 242.

40. Ibid.

Kong are operators, fabricators and laborers.[41] The USA Census Bureau reports in 2010 that 51.5 percent of Chinese and 74.1 percent of Taiwanese in USA (aged of 25 or older) are with college or higher education, while 19.3 percent of Chinese and 4.8 percent of Taiwanese have less than high school diploma. The same source also shows that in 2010, 52 percent of migrants or immigrants from China have management, business, science and arts occupations, while 20 percent of them have service occupations.[42] From this data, we can see the majority of Chinese (including Taiwanese) immigrants in the USA are well-educated, white-collar workers and professionals. Thus, it implies that the majority of members in the Chinese church in the USA are middle class and with higher socioeconomic status. Unlike missionary churches in their homeland in the nineteenth and twentieth centuries, Chinese people who go to a Chinese church in the USA rarely do so for physical needs.

Geographic Location

According to the census data in 2000 and 2010, the largest Chinese settlements are on the East and West Coasts, a typical bicoastal settlement pattern. The eight biggest Chinese immigrant cities are New York, Los Angeles, San Francisco, Oakland, San Jose, Suburban New Jersey, Boston and Chicago.[43] The US Census Bureau (2010) reported that California and New York make up more than half of the population of Chinese immigrants in the USA: 36.2 percent and 15.4 percent each.[44]

State	California	New York	Texas	Other states	Total
Percentage of Chinese	36.2%	15.4%	4.6%	43.9%	100%

Table 3.4. Demography of Chinese Immigrants in USA according to 2010 US Census

---

41. Fan, "Chinese Americans," 267.

42. http://www.census.gov/newsroom/pdf/cspan_fb_slides.pdf   (accessed   8 January 2014).

43. Fan, "Chinese Americans," 271.

44. http://www.census.gov/prod/cen2010/briefs/c2010br-11.pdf, p. 18.

The information I collected from Chinese church directories somewhat reflects the kind of settlement pattern reported by the US Census Bureau 2010. To make comparison with the 2010 census data, I only focus on the three states: California, New York and Texas, which are the top states where Chinese immigrants dwell. From those 790 Chinese churches that I confirmed that are active, about 32.9 percent of Chinese churches are located in California and 9.6 percent in New York. While reflecting the general pattern of settlement as noted above, these percentages are also much lower than the population percentage. In the US Census Bureau's report, 4.6 percent of Chinese live in Texas, and yet about 8.4 percent of Chinese churches are located there (see table 3.4. above). From my confirmed list of Chinese churches, it also shows about half of Chinese churches in the USA are located in California, New York and Texas.

	California	New York	Texas	Other states	Total
Number of churches listed	260	76	66	388	**790**
Percent	32.9%	9.6%	8.4%	49.1%	**100%**

Table 3.5. Location of Chinese Churches according to My Confirmed List

The US Census Bureau reports that in 2010, 49 percent of Chinese live in the West, 26.4 percent in the Northeast, 15.7 percent in the South, and 8.9 percent in the Midwest.[45] From the response of the survey questionnaire, we found that the result somewhat agrees with the previous research data and the information of directories. I sent out questionnaires to 652 Chinese churches from my list, which have valid email addresses, and about 36.1 percent of the respondents are from the West Coast and about 30.4 percent from the East (Figure 3.1). But compared with the Chinese population census data, this result may also imply a higher churched rate in the Midwest and a lower churched rate in the West among Chinese diaspora.

---

45. Ibid.

Location of US Chinese Churches

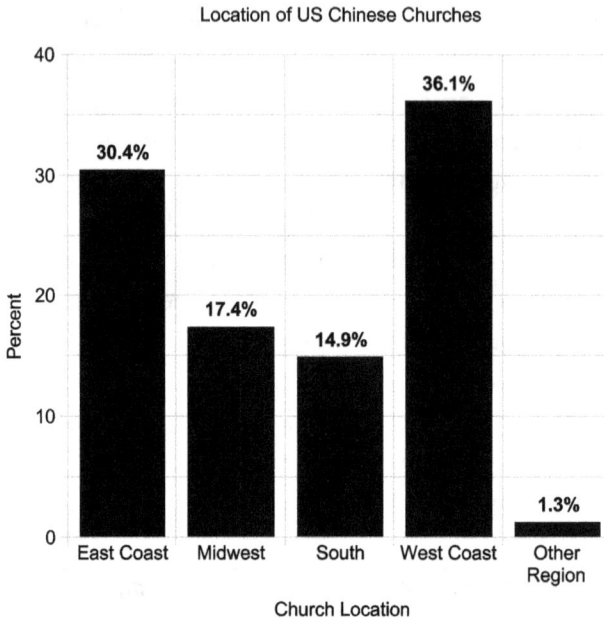

Figure 3.1. Location of US Chinese churches (N=316)

Denomination

The first Chinese church in the USA was started in 1853 in San Francisco by an American missionary and it was Presbyterian.[46] In the nineteenth century, Chinese churches in the USA, which were for the earlier Chinese immigrants in California, were supported by American denominations.[47] Today, from the directories of the Chinese churches I collected, about 59.5 percent of Chinese churches in the USA are non-denominational or independent churches. Previous research data also supports this result.[48] As for the denominational churches, Baptist tops the number, makes about 17.8 percent of the Chinese churches in the USA. In some southern states there is an even greater presence of Baptist churches. For example, in Texas, 30.3 percent of Chinese churches are Baptist, while non-denominational

---

46. Yang, *Chinese Christians in America*, 5.

47. For more a detailed history of Chinese churches in the USA, please see Yang, *Chinese Christians in America*, 5–7.

48. Yang, *Chinese Christians in America*, 7.

churches are still the majority, which make up 59.1 percent (see table 3.6). It is also remarkable that California and New York, the two major settlements of early Chinese immigrants in the nineteenth century, have a higher percentage of denominational Chinese churches (45.8% and 46.1%) than other states (35.8%). For those new Chinese immigrants who came to the USA after 1960s, many of them came as international students and became Christians through Bible study groups, and these fellowship groups eventually grew to independent/non-denominational churches in the 1980s and 1990s.[49] The data from analyzing the directories displays this phenomenon (see table 3.6 and figure 3.2).

	Non-denomination	Baptist	Other denominations	Total
California	141 (54.2%)	49 (18.9%)	70 (26.9%)	**260**
New York	41 (53.9%)	10 (13.2%)	25 (32.9%)	**76**
Texas	39 (59.1%)	20 (30.3%)	7 (10.6%)	**66**
Other states	249 (64.2%)	62 (16.0%)	77 (19.8%)	**388**
USA	470 (59.5%)	141 (17.8%)	179 (22.7%)	**790**

Table 3.6. Summary of the Relation between Denomination and Location

---

49. Ling, *The "Chinese Way,"* 92.

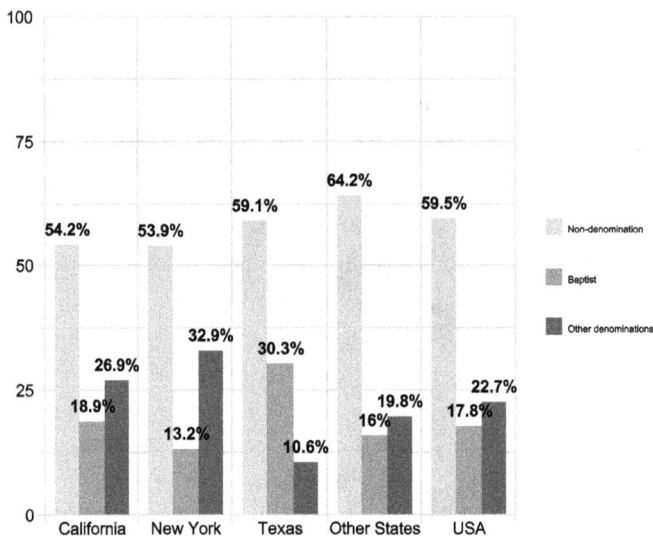

Figure 3.2. Denominations of Chinese Churches in Different States (N=790)

The result of the survey questionnaire agrees with the information from the directories. In the questionnaire, I added the two options, "Bread of Life Christian Church" and "Evangelical Formosan Church," and yet these two are not denominations, but branches of their mother churches in Taiwan. Thus, these two are counted as non-denominational churches (see figure 3.3 and table 3.7). In this way, it shows about 56.2 percent of the respondents are from non-denominational churches, and about 20.8 percent of the respondents are from Baptist churches (see figure 3.3 for the ranking of different affiliations of Chinese churches). This result is close to the data from the church list (59.5% and 17.8% respectively), which means these statistics accurately represent the Chinese churches in the USA, confirming the reliability of the result of this survey. The third largest denomination is Christian and Missionary Alliance (C&MA), which also agrees with previous research data.[50]

---

50. Yang, *Chinese Christians in America*, 7.

Congregation's Current Denominational Affiliation

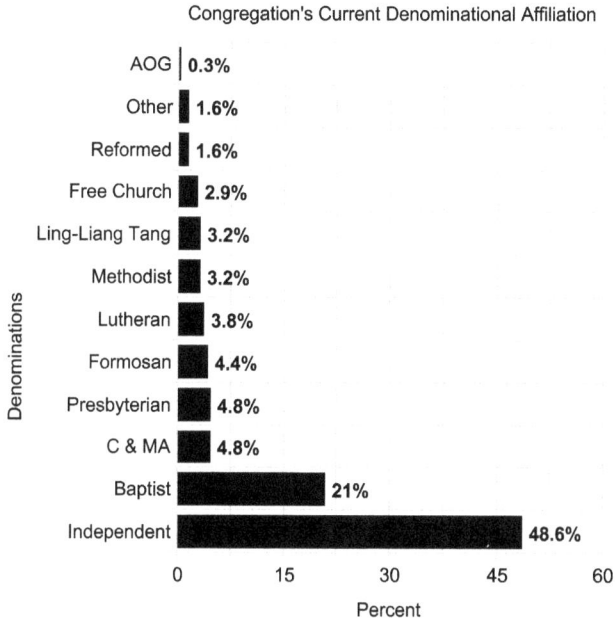

Denomination	Percent
AOG	0.3%
Other	1.6%
Reformed	1.6%
Free Church	2.9%
Ling-Liang Tang	3.2%
Methodist	3.2%
Lutheran	3.8%
Formosan	4.4%
Presbyterian	4.8%
C & MA	4.8%
Baptist	21%
Independent	48.6%

Figure 3.3. Affiliations of Chinese Churches in the USA (N=315)

Affiliations of Chinese Churches in the USA	Frequency	Percent (N=315)
The Assemblies of God	1	.3
Baptist Church	66	21.0
Bread of Life Christian Church (Ling-Liang Tang)*	10	3.2*
Christian and Missionary Alliance (C&MA)	15	4.8
Evangelical Formosan Church*	14	4.4*
Evangelical Free Church	9	2.9
Lutheran Church	12	3.8
Methodist Church	10	3.2
Reformed Church	5	1.6
Presbyterian Church	15	4.8
Non-denominational/Inter-denominational/ Independent Church*	153	48.6*
Sub Total	**310**	**98.6**
Church of the Nazarene	1	0.3
Evangelical Covenant Church	1	0.3
Evangelical Friends	1	0.3
First Evangelical Church Association	1	0.3
United Church of Christ	1	0.3
Sub Total Other Denominations	**5**	**1.5**
TOTAL	**315**	**100.0**

*Table 3.7. Denominations Reported by the Respondents (*Non-denomination)*

If we look at the denomination map through different regions of the USA, it shows the strong influence of Baptists in the South (see figure 3.6), and the lower percentage of non-denominational/independent churches on the West Coast (see figure 3.7). This result is close to the analysis of the Chinese churches list, and also agrees with the previous study and findings that suggest the areas with larger earlier Chinese immigrant populations have more denominational churches, since the new immigrants usually started their churches from Bible study groups and eventually became independent churches.[51] The data of the East Coast does not show this kind of result. One of the possible reasons can be that only New York is a settlement of earlier immigrants, while there are many other states in the East Coast which host new immigrants.

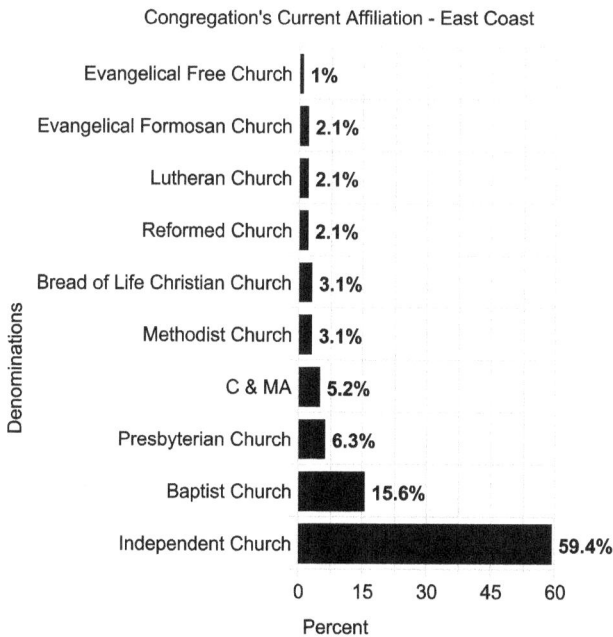

Congregation's Current Affiliation - East Coast

Denomination	Percent
Evangelical Free Church	1%
Evangelical Formosan Church	2.1%
Lutheran Church	2.1%
Reformed Church	2.1%
Bread of Life Christian Church	3.1%
Methodist Church	3.1%
C & MA	5.2%
Presbyterian Church	6.3%
Baptist Church	15.6%
Independent Church	59.4%

Figure 3.4. Denominations on the East Coast (N=96)

---

51. Ling, *The "Chinese Way,"* 92.

Congregation's Current Affiliation - Midwest

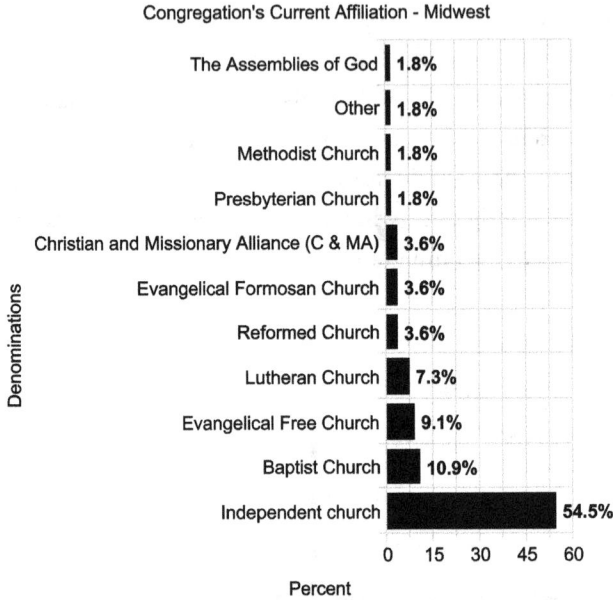

Figure 3.5. Denominations in the Midwest (N=55)

Congregation's Current Affiliation - South

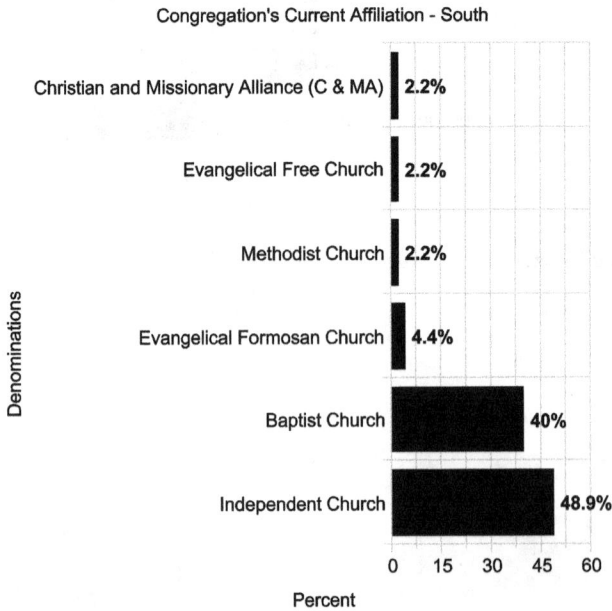

Figure 3.6. Denominations in the South (N=45)

Congregation's Current Affiliation - West Coast

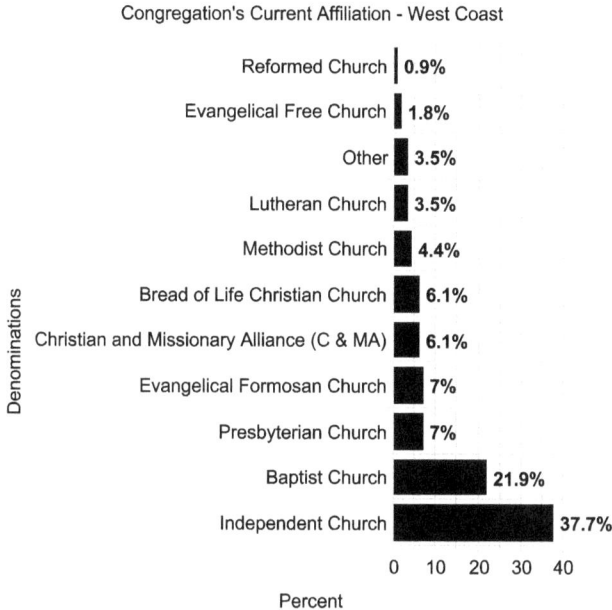

Figure 3.7. Denominations on the West Coast (N=114)

Congregation

US Chinese churches understand the term *congregation* slightly differently from general American churches. Congregation means "a group of people assembled for worship." In the American context, a different congregation means a different church, while in Chinese American churches, one church may have several congregations. These congregations are divided according to dialect, yet they all belong to one Chinese church. From previous stud- ies[52] and general observations, we know most of the attendees of Chinese churches are either immigrants or migrants from mainland China, Hong Kong, Taiwan, Southeast Asia and descendants of Chinese immigrants born in USA. As Yang mentioned in his research, "many scholars agree that the Chinese language is a strong factor upholding Chinese cultural unity."[53] The languages they use for Sunday service at church illustrate this

---

52. E.g. J. C. Ma and Carolyn Cartier, eds., *The Chinese Diaspora: Space, Place, Mobility, and Identity* (Lanham, MD: Roman & Littlefield, 2003); Yang, *Chinese Christians in America*; Wang, *The Chinese Overseas*.

53. Yang, *Chinese Christians in America*, 49.

fact well. Mandarin is the official language in the PRC and Taiwan, while
Cantonese is the mother tongue of the earlier immigrants originally from
Canton (Guangdong) in the nineteenth century[54] as well as people who are
from Hong Kong. Some of the early immigrants in Taiwan and Southeast
Asia, who originally were from Hokkien (Fujian) province and later re-migrated to the USA after the 1960s, speak Hokkienese/Taiwanese.[55] Usually
Chinese churches in the USA have more than one congregation, and they
separate the congregations according to their mother tongues. Whether
they speak Mandarin, Cantonese, Taiwanese or other Chinese dialects, the
written language is the same. However, the PRC developed the simplified
Chinese (written form), while Chinese diaspora in Taiwan, Hong Kong
and North America still use traditional Chinese. Most of the characters
of these two written forms are similar enough to be recognized by both
readers. When I was analyzing the web page of all Chinese churches in
the USA, I found out most Chinese churches' web pages are in traditional
Chinese or with an English version. Some of them have three versions:
English, traditional Chinese and simplified Chinese. Very few are only in
English or simplified Chinese. Thus in this questionnaire, the Chinese language was printed in traditional Chinese.

---

54. Ibid., 36.

55. Carolyn Cartier, "Diaspora and Social Restructuring in Postcolonial Malaysia," in
The Chinese Diaspora: Space, Place, Mobility, and Identity, ed. J. C. Ma and Carolyn Cartier
(Lanham, MD: Roman & Littlefield, 2003), 76.

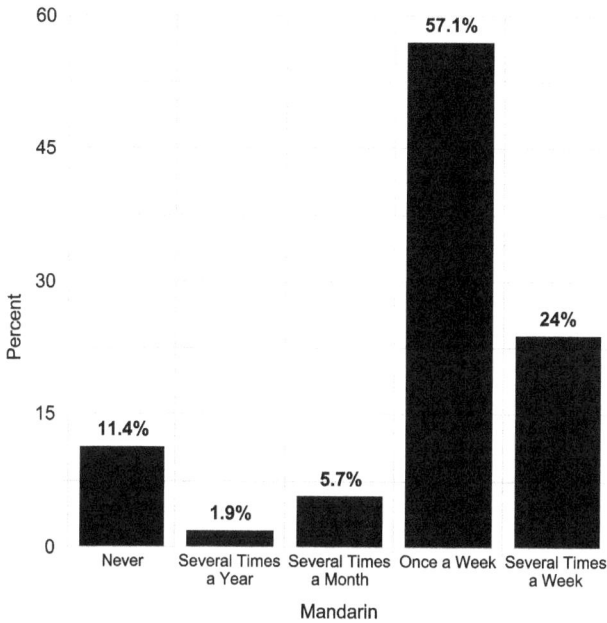

Figure 3.8. Frequency of Preaching in Mandarin among Chinese Churches (N=317)

From the result of the survey, Mandarin and English are the most frequently used languages in Chinese churches in the United States. Considering the frequency, about 81.1 percent of churches which responded to the survey have services in Mandarin once, or more than once, a week (see figure 3.8), and about 62.5 percent of the responding churches have services in English once, or more than once, a week (see figure 3.9). As for the number of churches that holds services in particular languages, out of 317 responding churches there are 280 holding English services and 281 holding Mandarin services. The third is Cantonese, with 108 churches holding services in this language (see figure 3.10).

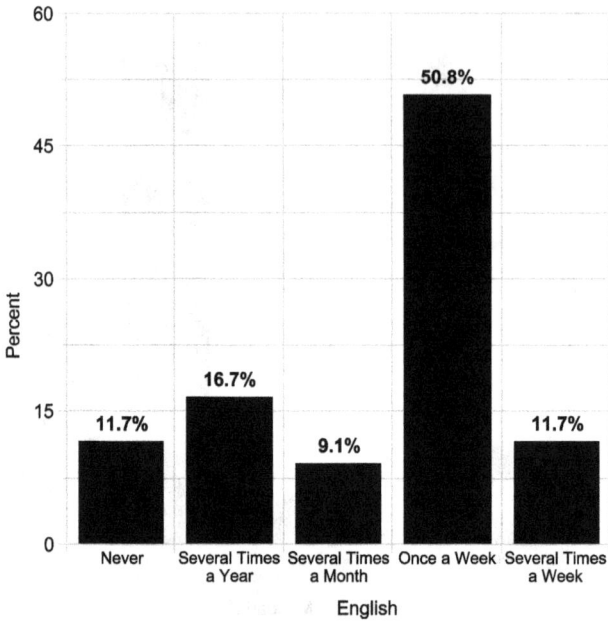

Figure 3.9. Frequency of Preaching in English among Chinese Churches (N=317)

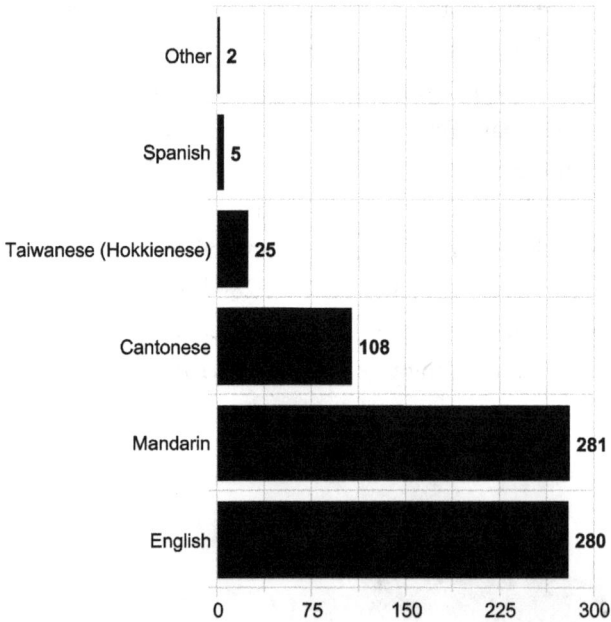

Figure 3.10. The Number of Churches Having Services in the Listed Languages

As for the size of each congregation, the survey data shows that Mandarin congregations hold the largest services, with average 128.65 weekly attendees, and English is the second, with 91.14 (see figure 3.11). The research result implies that the majority of attendees of Chinese churches in the USA are relatively recent immigrants whose first language is Mandarin. If we focus on Cantonese, which is the mother tongue of the earlier Chinese immigrants in nineteenth century, the data shows that in the West Coast – where the earlier Chinese immigrants settled – the percentage of Cantonese congregations is much higher than any other regions in the USA (see table 3.8). These results agree with previous research, as Yang points out in his study that "over 90 percent of Chinese Protestant churches have been founded by post-1965 immigrants, a majority of whom are educated Chinese from all over China and Southeast Asia."[56]

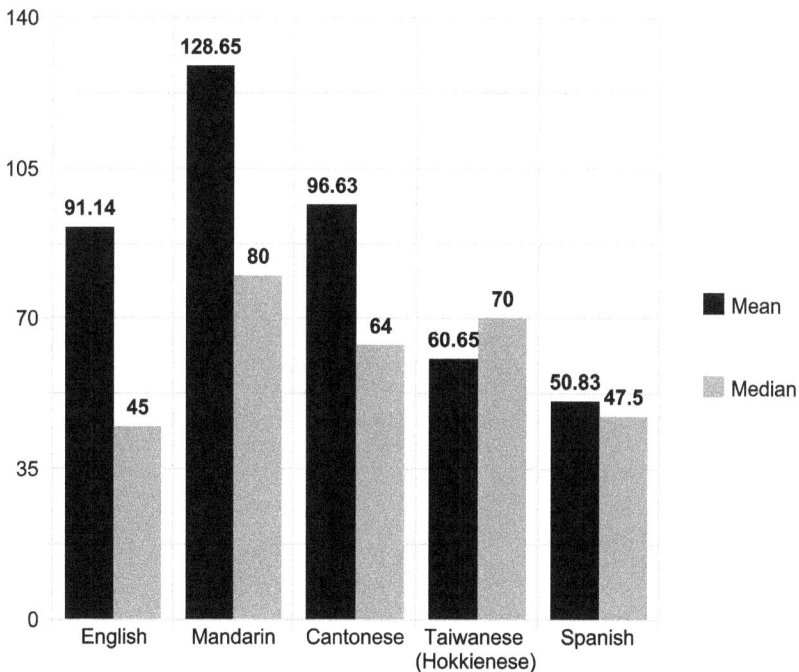

Figure 3.11. The Mean and Median of Attendees of Each Service

56. Fenggang Yang, "Gender and Generation in a Chinese Christian Church," in *Asian American Religions: The Making and Remaking of Border and Boundaries*, ed. Tony Carnes and Fenggang Yang (New York: New York University Press, 2004), 210.

Frequency of Service in Cantonese	East Coast (N=96)	Midwest (N=55)	South (N=47)	West Coast (N=114)
Never	66.7%	69.1%	72.3%	62.3%
Several times a year	7.3%	5.5%	6.4%	0
Several times a month	3.1%	5.5%	2.1%	1.8%
Once a week	18.7%	14.5%	17.0%	27.2%
Several times a week	4.2%	5.5%	2.1%	8.8%

Table 3.8. Summary of the Relation between Location and Service in Cantonese

As for the size of Chinese churches in the USA, the data shows that the average total weekly attendance (including adults and children) is 248, and the median Chinese church in the USA has 125 attendees on the Sunday worship service (see table 3.9). More than half (52.3%) of Chinese churches have a weekly attendance of 76–250 people (see figure 3.12). We can compare this with the all of USA churches, which have 186 average attendees according to USCLS survey of the year of 2008/2009, and the median USA church has 75 regular attendees on the Sunday worship, according to 2009 data of National Congregations Study (NCS). NCS also reports that 59 percent of USA churches are in the size of 799, while 2.4 percent of them are larger than the size of 1,000.[57] This data shows that most Chinese churches are of similar size, unlike other American churches, with some megachurches which are 1,000 plus or even 10,000 plus and on the other hand with most other churches being very small. In addition, considering the average size, Chinese churches are larger, on average, than general American churches.

---

57. http://hirr.hartsem.edu/research/fastfacts/fast_facts.html#sizecong (accessed 15 April 2014).

	Attendees of US Chinese Churches	Attendees of All US Churches
Number of Churches	315	about 314,000
Mean	247.95	186
Median	125.00	75
Mode	100	n/a
Minimum	15	7
Maximum	2,800	More than 10,000
Sum	78,103	About 56,000,000

Table 3.9. Comparison of the Size of US Chinese Churches and All US Churches (US church data from NCS study 2009 and USCLS 2009).

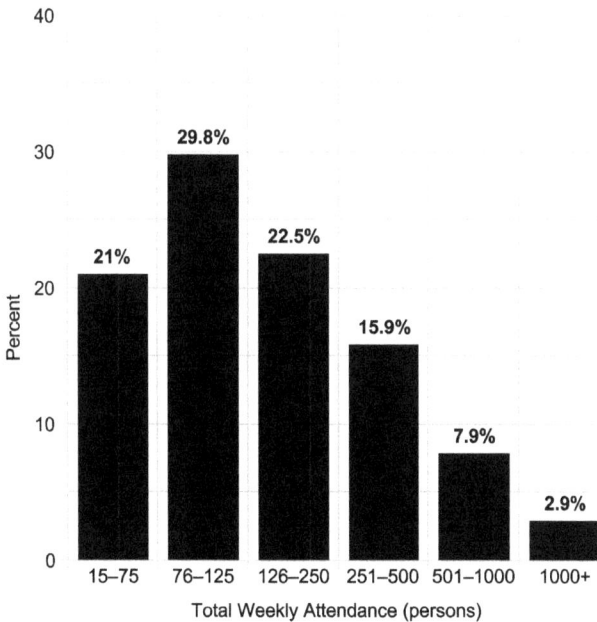

Figure 3.12. Total Weekly Attendance of Chinese Churches (N=315)

Church Leadership

Rev Tzeng-Ching Chen analyzed the leadership structure of Chinese churches in the USA in his article: "There are normally three kinds of authorities in the Chinese church in the USA: the clergy, deacon or/and elder board, and the professionals. The clergy has spiritual authority, deacons or/and elders hold the power of decision making, and the professionals also have authority because of their abundant knowledge."[58] From previous research data, more than half of Chinese churches in the USA started from student Bible groups and do not have a denominational background, so they are not planted by American missionaries or clergy, and it is not uncommon that these student leaders (after they graduated and had a career in the USA) later became the church leaders, namely, pastors, elders or deacons.[59] Thus, their leadership tends to be congregational,[60] and the founding members may feel they have some sort of authority in this church. In the light of this, this research targets the pastors, elders and deacons of Chinese churches in USA to respond to the questionnaire.

---

58. Tzeng-Ching Chen, "Challenge and Solution: A Discussion on Chinese Church in North America" (挑戰與因應之道－－論北美華人教會), *Ambassadors Magazine* (使者雜誌), 9/10 (1997), http://soareagle55.wordpress.com/2008/10/26, (accessed 1 October 2010).

59. Ling, *The "Chinese Way,"* 92.

60. Chen, "Challenge and Solution."

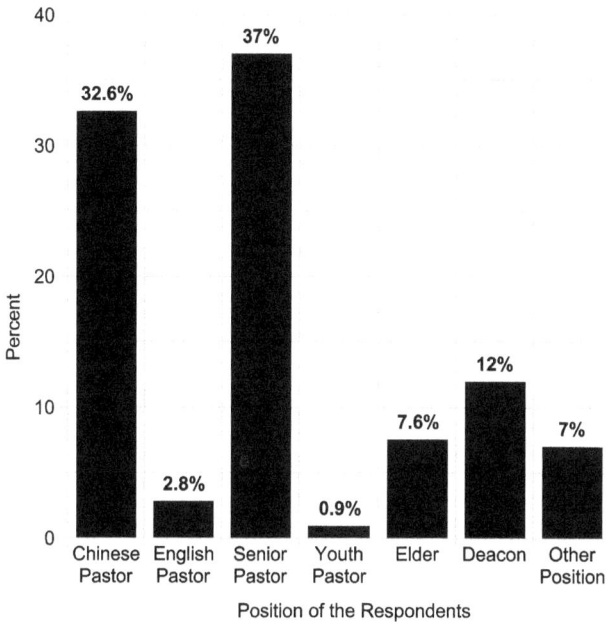

Figure 3.13. The Positions of the Respondents (N=316)

This survey requested church leaders to respond to the questionnaire. I gave the choices of senior pastors, Chinese (Mandarin or dialects) pastors, English pastors and youth pastors based on the observation of Chinese church websites. These are the most common pastoral positions offered by Chinese churches in the USA. From the research data, about 93.7 percent of the respondents are pastors, elders and deacons (see figure 3.13), which includes senior pastors (37%), Chinese pastors (32.6%), deacons (12%) elders (7.6%), and one children's pastor (0.3%) and one mission pastor (0.3%) who answered "other position." For the other respondents who answered "other position" (7%), 2.2 percent of them are an administrator or church secretary, 1.9 percent are a co-worker, coordinator, leader or church council person and the rest of the respondents provided very diverse answers (see table 3.10).

Other positions	Frequency	Percent
Administrator/church secretary	7	2.2
Children's pastor	1	0.3
Co-worker/coordinator/leader/church council	6	1.9
Founder	1	0.3
Layman	2	0.6
Lead servant of Chinese ministry	1	0.3
Mission pastor	1	0.3
Missions Committee lay member	1	0.3
Principal co-worker	1	0.3
Tentmaker	1	0.3
Total	**22**	**7**

Table 3.10. Other Answers of Position Provided by the Respondents

According to the data of the US Immigration and Naturalization Service in 2002, most of Chinese immigrants are born in China: 45,652 of Chinese immigrants are from mainland China, while 5,419 are from Hong Kong, and 9,040 are from Taiwan. In other words, about three-quarters of Chinese immigrants are from mainland China.[61] More recent data from the US Immigration and Naturalization Service in reports that 33,966 came from mainland China in 2010, and 31,868 in 2012. Hong Kong and Taiwan are not in the list since the naturalized persons are less than 9,000.[62] However, the result of this survey shows that leadership does not present this kind of demographic. The data shows 40.7 percent of the respondents are from Taiwan, about 24.4 percent are from mainland China and about 18.9 percent from Hong Kong (see figure 3.14).

---

61. Fan, "Chinese Americans," 266.

62. Office of Immigration Statistics 2012, 2. The data in 2002 is more relevant in this case when considering the Chinese church leadership because usually Chinese church leaders have immigrated in USA for years, less likely in 2010 or 2012.

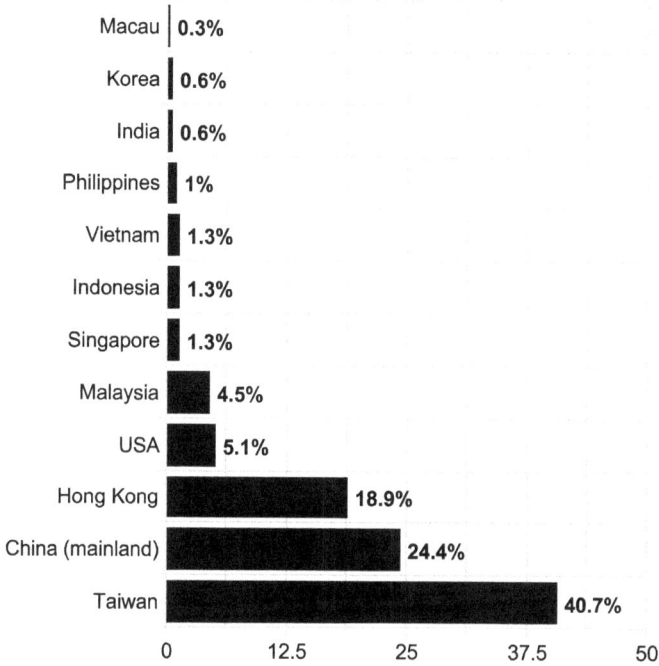

Figure 3.14. Birthplace of the Respondents (N=312)

In other words, more than half (59.6%) of the respondents, who are church leaders, are from either Taiwan or Hong Kong, and less than one-quarter are from mainland China. If we break down the data and merely see the case of pastors, the percentage of the pastors in Chinese churches from mainland China is even lower, and the percentage of pastors from Hong Kong is higher than from mainland China (see figure 3.15). This result agrees with the general perception in the Chinese church that most of the pastors in Chinese churches in the USA are either from Taiwan or Hong Kong.[63]

---

63. For example, every year there are several Chinese Christian conferences and retreat camps in different regions of USA, and the majority of the speakers are either from Taiwan or Hong Kong.

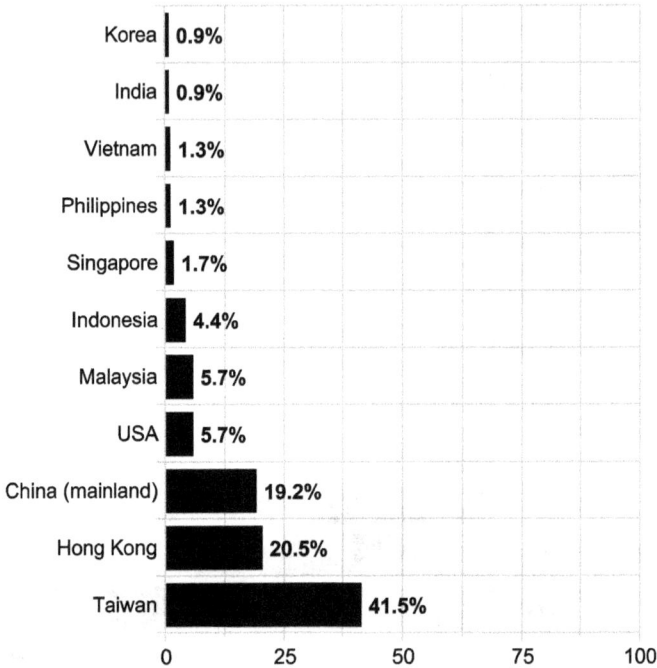

Figure 3.15. Birthplace of the Pastors (N=232)

One of the possible reasons that most leaders of Chinese churches in the USA are from Taiwan and Hong Kong is that Chinese immigrants from Taiwan and Hong Kong came earlier than those from the PRC. Immigrants from Taiwan and China had increased after the 1960s after the passage of the Immigration Act of 1965, while a large amount of Chinese students and scholars from mainland China started to come after the "Reform and Opening Up" of the PRC during the 1980s and 1990s.[64] The Taiwan Relation Act of 1979 also gave Taiwanese more opportunities of acquiring USA citizenship.[65] Since immigrants from Taiwan and Hong Kong came earlier and were often the founding members of Chinese churches, it is not surprising that many of them are also the leaders of church.

A good example is my home church in northern suburban Chicago. The church was started by a few professionals from Hong Kong about thirty

---

64. Wang and Yang, "Evangelical and Ethnic," 181.
65. Yang, Chinese Christians in America, 35.

years ago, and fifteen years later they started a Mandarin congregation to reach out to the new immigrants from mainland China. These founding members, who have stayed at this church longer than anyone else, are our elders and highly respected in our church.

In fact, it is not uncommon that in the Chinese churches in the USA, pastors come and go, while the elders or founding members always stay.[66] As I interviewed an elder from a Chinese church in the East Coast, he told me that in his church "elder is a life-long position." In this sense we have a clearer picture of the leadership structure of Chinese churches in United States.

Ethnicity	Frequency	Percent
Chinese	306	97.1
Non-Chinese Asian	4	1.3
Caucasian	4	1.3
Other (did not specify)	1	.3
Total	**315**	**100.0**

Table 3.11. Ethnicity of the Respondents

Other birth places	Frequency	Percent (N= 312)
India	2	0.6
Korea	2	0.6
Macau	1	0.3
Philippines	3	1.0
Vietnam	4	1.3
Total	**12**	**3.8**

Table 3.12. Other Birthplaces of the Respondents

---

66. Chen, "Challenge and Solution."

To make sure these church leaders from different parts of the world are mostly ethnic Chinese, the questionnaire includes this question regarding ethnicity. The result shows 97.1 percent of the respondents are ethnic Chinese (see table 3.11). Of those twelve born in other countries (see table 3.12), all of them, except for three (two born in Korea, one in India) self-identify as Chinese ethnically. Of those born in the USA, four out of sixteen self-identify as Caucasian. This data shows the diversity of Chinese diaspora churches in the USA in light of the diversity of birthplaces of the church leaders. Although these Chinese church leaders are from different countries, they all can read and write either Chinese or English, and more than half of them chose to answer the questionnaire in Chinese (see table 3.13). The data also shows there is no significant difference on the positions they serve and church location between respondents who answered in English and Chinese. Yet a higher percentage of respondents who answered in Chinese are from Taiwan (51.4%).

Survey language	Frequency	Percent
Chinese	180	56.8
English	137	43.2
Total	**317**	**100.0**

Table 3.13. Preferred Language for the Survey

Previous research shows that mission pastors are the key people in US megachurches promoting missions and organizing mission programs such as mission conferences, short-term mission trips, etc.[67] Based on my observation and analysis on the web pages of all Chinese churches in the USA, very few (about 1%) of them have the position of mission pastor, thus there is no option of "mission pastor" in that question regarding position. The result of the survey agrees with this observation: among those who answer "other position," only one of the twenty-two put "mission pastor." In other words, out of the 316 respondents of this question, only one is a mission pastor, and the percentage is 0.3 percent. We can compare this with the

---

67. Priest, Wilson and Johnson, "U.S. Megachurches," 102.

survey on STM among megachurches in the USA, in which 73 percent of the respondents identified themselves as mission pastors.[68] Although almost all of these respondents from Chinese churches are not mission pastors, the data reports that 74.1 percent of them have gone on short-term mission trips (see table 3.14), and among those who have gone for short-term missions, more than one-fifth of them have gone more than ten times (see figure 3.16). If we break down the data and see only the case of pastors, it shows 86.1 percent of the pastors in Chinese churches have gone on short-term missions (see table 3.15). This proves the general idea that pastors are part of the short-term mission movement of Chinese churches in the United States.

Personal STM	Frequency	Percent
No	73	25.9
Yes	209	74.1
Total	**282**	**100.0**

Table 3.14. Personal STM Experiences of the Respondents

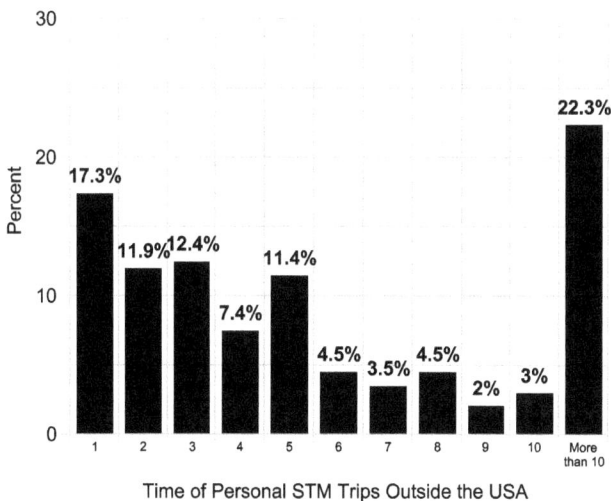

Figure 3.16. Numbers of Overseas STM Trips of Respondents (N=202)

---

68. Ibid., 101.

Pastors' STM	Frequency	Percent
No	29	13.9
Yes	179	86.1
Total	**208**	**100.0**

Table 3.15. Pastors' STM Experiences

Furthermore, according to the result of this survey, about 65.2 percent of Chinese churches have held a mission conference at least once, and 42.7 percent of Chinese churches hold a mission conference every year (see figure 3.17). This result suggests that although they do not have the title "mission pastor," Chinese church leaders are generally involved in mission programs. It also implies that compared with US megachurches, Chinese churches in the USA present a different kind of leadership culture in the way of doing missions.

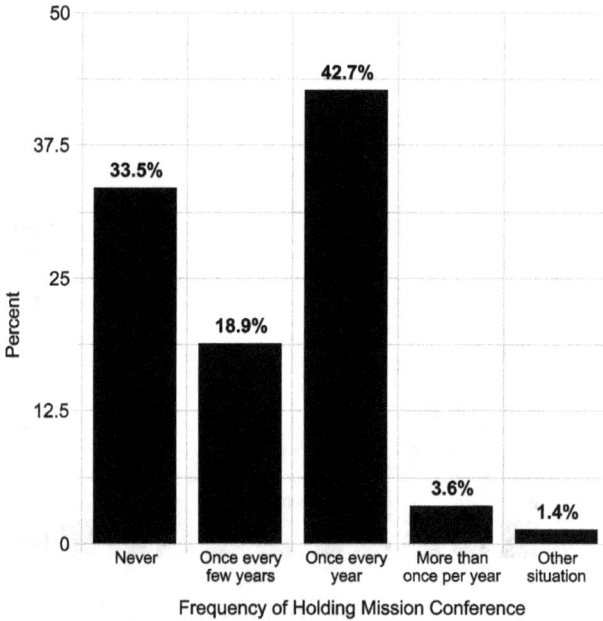

Figure 3.17. Frequency of Holding Mission Conferences (N=281)

We have looked at the demographics, denomination, congregation and leadership of the US Chinese church, a general understanding of transnationalism among Chinese people in the USA, and the research methods used to study the phenomena of US Chinese mission. Next, we turn to the research results, analyzing the way US Chinese churches practice mission, and how these churches exemplify "mission through diaspora."

CHAPTER 4

Analyzing Diaspora Mission
in Chinese Context

How do US Chinese churches carry out mission? Our research data paints a picture which helps answer this question. This chapter focuses on the general mission activities of the US Chinese church, while the next chapter focuses specifically on their short-term mission practice.

From the data collected by the questionnaire survey, we gain a basic idea of the mission involvement of the Chinese diaspora in the United States. Out of the 236 responding churches, the average (mean) money for overseas ministries is about $51,964 and the average percentage of the church expenditures for overseas ministries is about 11.9 percent. Most (about 46.5%) of Chinese churches' mission expenditures are between 6 and 15 percent (see figure 4.1). The proportion of total annual expenditures on overseas ministries of US Chinese churches is quite similar to US megachurches. Though much smaller in size (see figure 3.12), Chinese churches even have a slightly higher percentage for overseas ministry budget than US megachurches (about 10%). From previous research data,[1] 35.3 percent of the US megachurches' annual overseas ministry expenditures is 0–5 percent, and only 18.1 percent of them have overseas expenditures higher than 15 percent, while 23 percent of Chinese churches' expenditures on overseas ministry is 0–5 percent, and 31.9 percent of them is higher than 15 percent (see table 4.1).

---

1. Priest, Wilson, and Johnson, "U.S. Megachurches," 97.

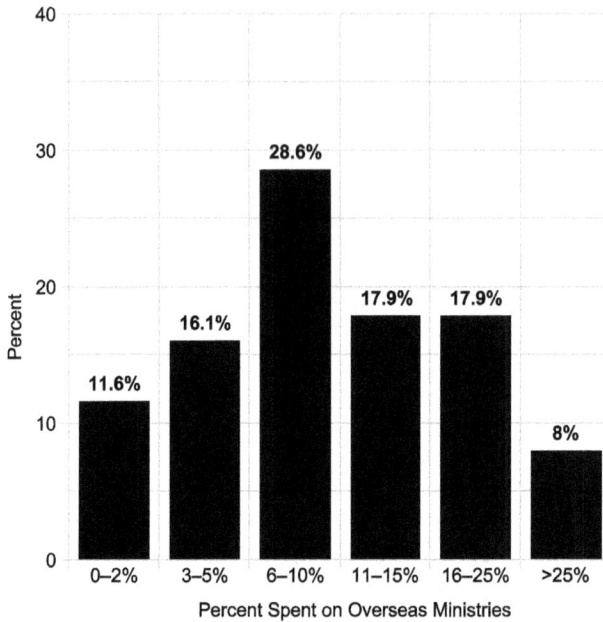

Figure 4.1. Percentage of Budget Spent on Overseas Ministries (N=224)

Percent Spent Overseas	Chinese Churches (percent)	Megachurch (percent)
0–2%	11.6	15.2
3–5%	16.1	20.1
6–10%	28.6	30.4
11–15%	17.9	16.3
16–25%	17.9	12.9
>25%	8.0	5.2
Total	**100.0**	**100.0**

Table 4.1. Comparison of Chinese Church and Megachurch on Overseas Ministry Budget

It is interesting that the statistic data of Chinese churches in the US does show that there is a positive correlation (r= 0.183, $p < 0.01$) between church size and the percentage of money spent on overseas ministries,[2] (i.e. the larger the Chinese church is, the more likely they spend a higher percent on overseas missions). Yet, although US megachurches are much larger in size compared with average Chinese churches, the percentage spent on overseas ministries is not higher than Chinese churches. This research result suggests that the Chinese churches in the US are just as involved in overseas missions as US megachurches, even though much smaller in size and financial ability. But in what kind of overseas ministries do Chinese churches invest their resources? This is the topic we discuss in the following sections.

"Chinese First" Missiology

National Chinese and diaspora Chinese together are 1.4 billion people, which makes one-fifth of the world's population. Regarding the large Chinese population in the world and China as the largest World B country, it makes sense that overseas Chinese Christians believe they have the responsibility to reach out to their own people first. Yang mentioned the "Chinese first" principle of ministry in his book *Chinese Christians in America*, finding that this is a common idea among Chinese churches in his research.[3] The result of my quantitative research also supports this general idea. On the questions related to prioritized concern of their churches, the choice "missions to Chinese" scores highest, and about 73 percent of responding churches choose this as their top priority (see figure 4.2).

---

2. Pearson Correlation.
3. Yang, *Chinese Christians in America*, 174.

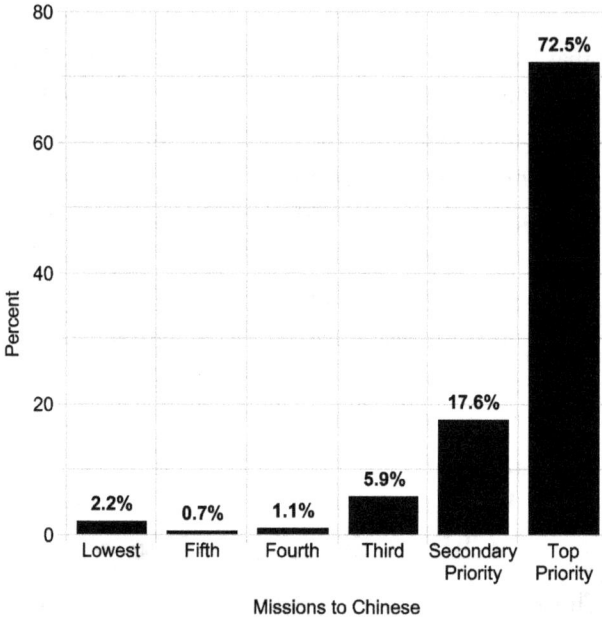

Figure 4.2. Prioritized Ministry as Missions to Chinese (N=273)

While previous studies[4] report that the top priority for US megachurch-es and US Korean churches is "missions to 'the unreached'" (see table 4.2), this study shows that this is a secondary priority for Chinese churches in the United States. Only 28 percent of Chinese churches report "missions to the unreached" as their top priority, while 33.6 percent of them choose this as their secondary priority (see figure 4.3). Besides "missions to Chinese," Chinese churches' top two and top three are the same with the top one and top two of Korean churches and megachurches in the USA – "missions to the unreached" and "church planting" – and for all of them "theological education" is the fourth priority (see figure 4.4). It is interesting to see gen-erally that churches in the USA have similar prioritized concerns, e.g. reach the unreached and church planting, but Chinese churches seem to have much stronger concerns for their own kinsmen's salvation compared with Korean churches according to the research result. Since South Korea is less

---

4. Priest, Wilson, and Johnson, "U.S. Megachurches," 97; Sokpyo Hong, "The Impact of Short-Term Mission Trips on Interracial and Interethnic Attitudes among Korean American Church Members," PhD diss., Trinity International University, 2011, 88.

of an unreached country, it will be interesting to see what the result would be if some future research puts "missions to North Koreans" as an option.

	US Korean Church	US Megachurch	US Chinese Church
Top priority **Lowest priority**	• Missions to the unreached • Church planting • Poverty relief • Theological education abroad • Evangelizing the Muslim world • Medical missions • Racial reconciliation • Social justice • Bible translation • AIDS in Africa	• Missions to the unreached • Church planting • Evangelizing the Muslim world • Theological education • Medical missions • Poverty relief • Bible translation • Racial reconciliation • AIDS in Africa • Social justice	• Missions to Chinese • Missions to the unreached • Church planting • Theological education abroad • Poverty relief • Medical missions • Evangelizing the Muslim world • Bible translation • Social justice • Racial reconciliation • AIDS in Africa

Table 4.2. Comparison of Ministry Priority among Megachurch, Korean Church and Chinese Church.[5]

---

5. Korean data from Hong 2011; megachurch data from Priest, Wilson, and Johnson "U.S. Megachurches."

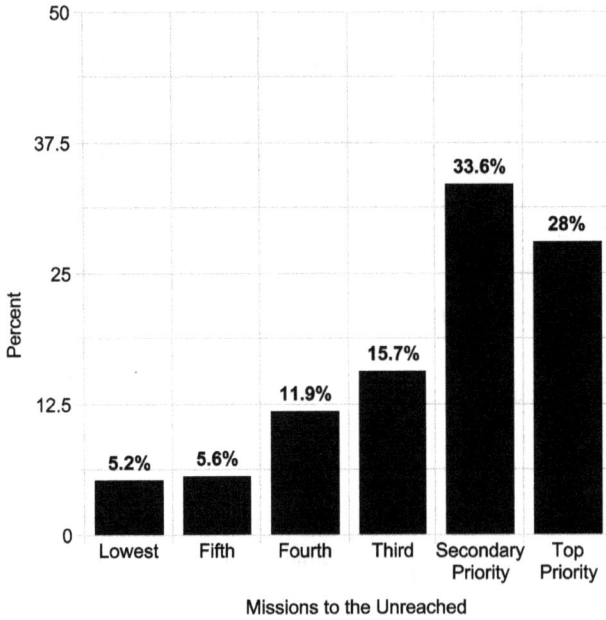

Figure 4.3. Prioritized Ministry as Missions to Unreached (N=268)

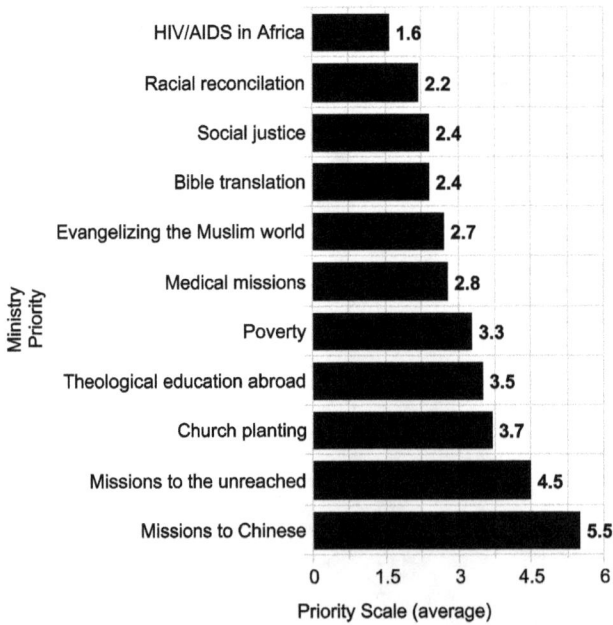

Figure 4.4. Ministry Priority (lowest: 1, highest: 6)

As for supporting long-term missionaries, 50 percent of Chinese churches are supporting 1 to 5 overseas long-term missionaries, and about 20.1 percent of them do not support long-term missionaries outside of the United States. Compared with megachurches in the USA – 41.5 percent of them support 11 to 40 long-term missionaries and only 6 percent do not support any missionaries.[6] This is a much smaller number. But we need to remember the size of Chinese churches is also much smaller, and thus the financial resources are smaller accordingly. The data also shows that there is a strong and significant positive correlation between the church size and the number of overseas long-term missionaries ($r = 0.593$, $p < 0.01$).[7] It means the larger the church is, the more long-term missionaries the church supports.

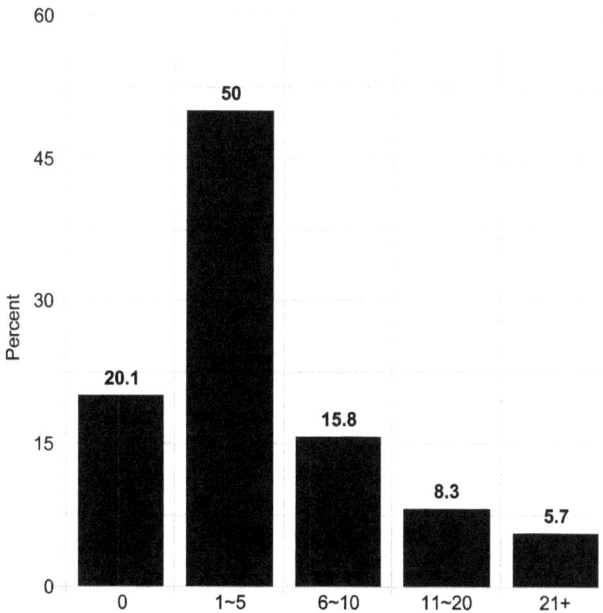

Figure 4.5. Percentage of the Number of Long-Term Overseas Missionaries Supported by US Chinese Church (N=278)

---

6. Priest, Wilson and Johnson, "U.S. Megachurches," 98.
7. Pearson Correlation.

When asking further in which region their long-term missionaries are serving, from the 222 Chinese churches that are supporting long-term overseas missionaries, 206 of them report that they are supporting long-term missionaries in Asia (see figure 4.6). A note here is that one church can support multiple missionaries in different regions, and thus this is not a single choice. The data shows that among the 206 churches supporting long-term missionaries in Asia, 177 of them are supporting missionaries in ethnic Chinese areas like mainland China, Hong Kong, Macau, Singapore and Taiwan. In other words, at least 177 of the responding churches are supporting long-term missionaries in ethnic Chinese countries or areas, and China is the top place their long-term missionaries are serving: 169 of the responding churches support missionaries there (see table 4.3).

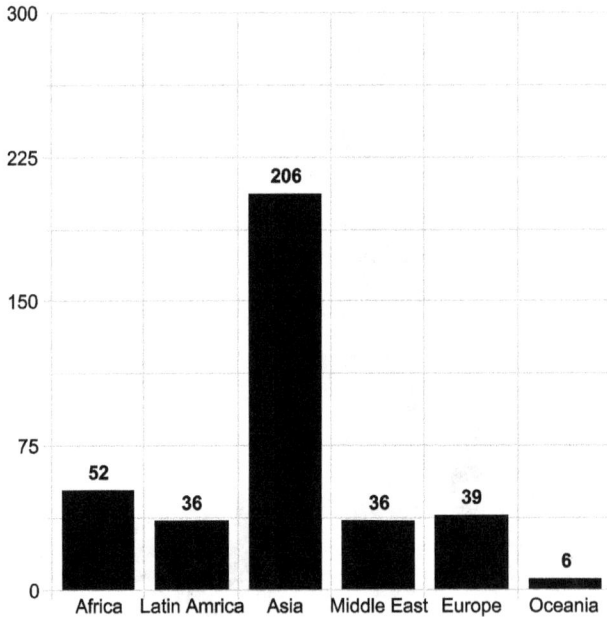

Figure 4.6. The Number of Churches Supporting Long-Term Missionaries in the Listed Regions

	Mainland China	Mainland China, Hong Kong, Macau, Singapore, Taiwan	Asia (excluding Middle East)
Number of churches supporting missionaries in the listed areas	169	177	206

Table 4.3. Analysis of Long-Term Missionaries' Mission Field

When asking how many of the long-term missionaries whom their churches support are serving/reaching out to ethnic Chinese, about 27.5 percent of the responding churches answer "all of them," and about 31.1 percent answer "most of them" (see figure 4.7).

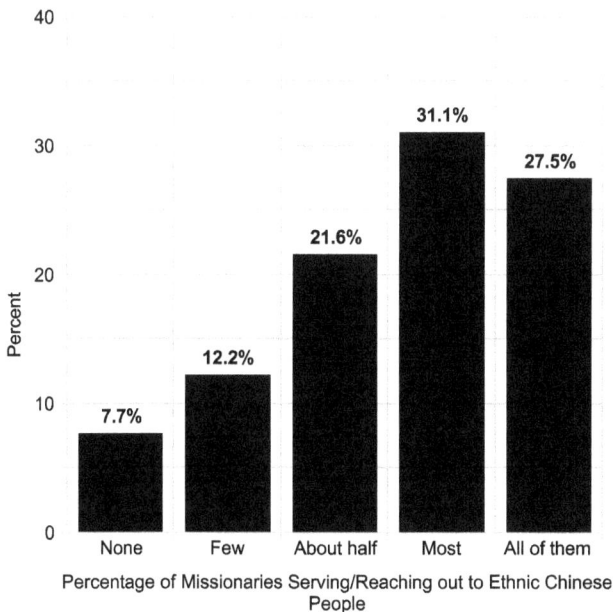

Figure 4.7. Percentage of Missionaries Serving Ethnic Chinese (N=222)

If we focus on those sixty-one churches that answer "all of their long-term missionaries are ministering to ethnic Chinese" and see where their long-term missionaries serve, we find out twelve of these churches support missionaries in Africa, Latin America and Europe (see figure 4.8). Among the fifty-eight churches that support missionaries in Asia, three of them are supporting missionaries in Thailand, Myanmar, Philippines and Indonesia; the rest of them are supporting missionaries in Chinese countries or areas.

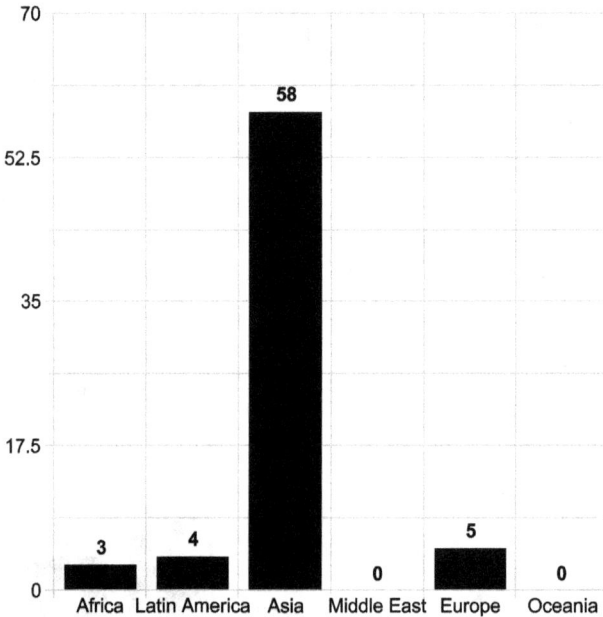

Figure 4.8. Number of Churches Supporting Long-Term Missionaries Who All Are Ministering to Ethnic Chinese in the Listed Regions

From this data, we can say that most Chinese churches are supporting long-term missionaries serving in Chinese societies, and even those missionaries who are not in Chinese societies may still be ministering to overseas Chinese.

As for the short-term missions, 151 out of the 180 Chinese churches that sent short-term mission teams in 2012 sent STM teams to Asia (see figure 4.9), and 134 out of these 151 churches sent at least one STM team to the area where the society is majority (ethnic) Chinese, e.g. mainland China, Hong Kong, Macau, Singapore and Taiwan. China is the top destination of the short-term mission trips: 103 Chinese churches at least sent one of their STM teams to China in 2012 (see table 4.4).

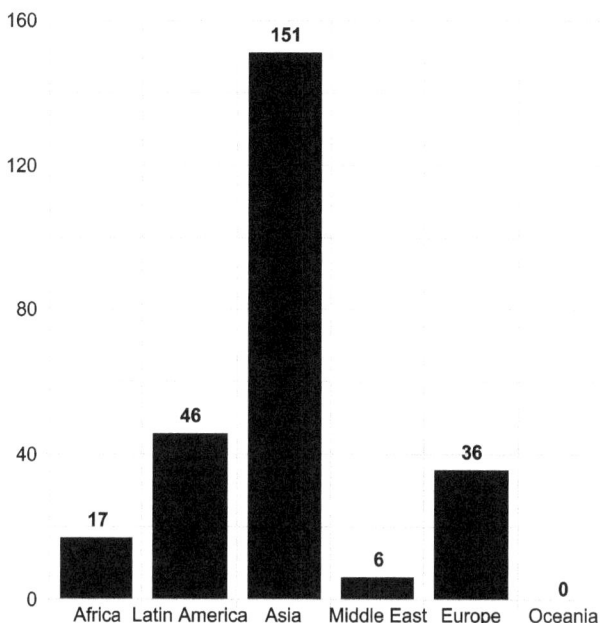

Figure 4.9. Number of Churches Sending STM to the Listed Regions

	Mainland China	Mainland China, Hong Kong, Macau, Singapore, Taiwan	Asia (excluding Middle East)
Number of churches sending STM teams to the listed areas	103	134	151

Table 4.4. Analysis of STM Team's Destinations

As for the people groups the STM teams serve, about 68.7 percent of the responding churches say their primary ministry is to "Chinese people," and about 22.3 percent say to "both Chinese and non-Chinese," and only 8.9 percent say to "non-Chinese" (see figure 4.10). Since about 74 percent of Chinese churches that sent STM teams in 2012 sent at least one of their teams to Chinese countries and areas (they may have also sent other teams to non-Chinese countries), it is reasonable that 68.7 percent of them report that their STM teams primarily ministered to ethnic Chinese. Are those churches sending their teams to non-Chinese countries also ministering to ethnic Chinese people? If we break down the data and see only the 123 churches whose primary ministry of STM is to ethnic Chinese, we find that although Asia is still the number one destination, there are also a good number of churches sending STM teams to Africa, Latin America and Europe to minister to overseas Chinese (see figure 4.11).

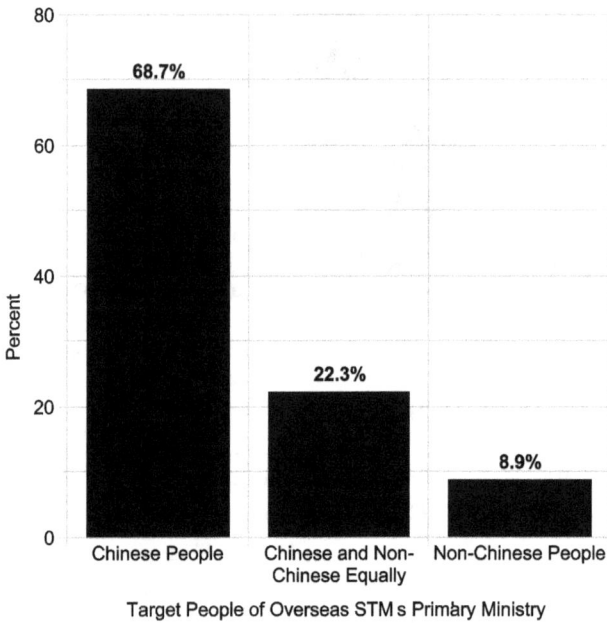

Figure 4.10. Those to Whom Overseas STMs Primarily Minister (N=179)

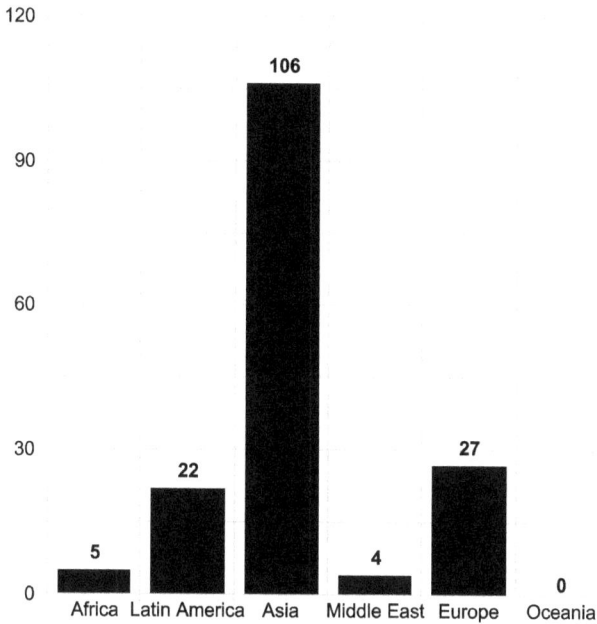

Figure 4.11. The Number of Churches' STM to the Regions Ministering Primarily to Ethnic Chinese

Social science studies often use correlation value to see how two variables relate to each other. In the previous section we use Pearson correlation, but here we use Spearman's Rho to find the correlation between the mission focus and mission priority of Chinese churches, because the data of this part of research is mostly ordinal.[8] This survey data shows a high percentage (72.5%) of Chinese churches in the USA that report that "mission to Chinese" is their top priority, and it is not surprising to see there are some correlations between "mission to Chinese" and both their long-term and short-term missions. The correlation value for Spearman's Rho shows that the churches which see "mission to Chinese" as a higher priority are more likely to support long-term missionaries who serve Chinese ($r= 0.174$, $p <0.05$), and less likely to send STM teams to minister to non-Chinese

---

8. "The Pearson correlation is used when you have two variables that are normal/scale, and the Spearman is used when one or both of the variables are ordinal" (George A. Morgan, Nancy L. Leech, Gene W. Gloeckner, Karen C. Barrett, *SPSS for Introductory Statistics: Use and Interpretation*, 3rd ed. [Mahwah, NJ: Lawrence Erlbaum, 2007], 117.).

(r= -0.277, p <0.01). The data also implies the ministry priority of "mission to Chinese" impacts the church's short-term mission even more significantly than their long-term missions.

Correlation with prioritized ministry as "mission to Chinese"	Spearman's Rho
How many of these long-term missionaries are serving/reaching out to ethnic Chinese people?	0.174*
The primary ministry for the STM teams in these countries/areas is to non-Chinese	-0.277**

Table 4.5. Correlation with Prioritized Ministry as "Mission to Chinese" (*Correlation is significant at the 0.05 level; **Correlation is significant at the 0.01 level.)

There is also a correlation between churches' long-term mission and short-term mission considering the target people: churches which support more long-term missionaries who serve Chinese are less likely to send STM teams to minister to non-Chinese (r= -0.291, p < 0.01). This correlation is even more significant, which suggests that churches' long-term missions have influence on their short-term mission regarding the target people, with the assumption that the short-term mission is a later or more recent activity in the church. From this research data, it shows that whether it is long-term or short-term mission, the Chinese church invests their resources mainly in overseas Chinese mission. This result agrees with the general impression that the mission activity of Chinese churches in the USA follows the principle of "Chinese first."

Chinese Diaspora Cooperation in Mission

Today, the best-trained diaspora Chinese Christians live in North America. As Wuthnow points out in his book, "Although the demographic center of gravity is shifting to the global South, the organizational and material resources of global Christianity remain heavily concentrated in the more affluent countries of North America and Europe."[9] Most mission work is

---

9. Wuthnow, *Boundless Faith*, 9.

supported by these people. For example, in the past two years I have been involved in a Chinese student ministry in Germany, but this ministry was founded in the USA by Chinese American Christians. Because American citizens can enter the European Union for three months without applying for a visa, it is convenient for Chinese American Christians to get involved in this type of short-term mission. When my coworkers arrived in Germany, Chinese Christian students who have been living in Germany for several years and studying in university there, hosted and took care of them. Because those Chinese students are familiar with German culture and language, they can help these coworkers from the USA get adjusted to the German culture.

When asking "who have their short-term mission teams collaborated with in the short-term mission in the most recent mission trip," for those 224 churches that sent short-term missions teams, 134 answered "local Chinese Christians from the mission field." The second is "Chinese Christians from USA" with 54 churches (see table 4.6). Since one short-term mission team can collaborate with different groups of people, their answers are multiple. This research data shows that most Chinese churches in the USA collaborate with other Chinese Christians in the mission field or from the USA in the short-term missions.

From the data of the previous section we see that these local Chinese Christians could be in non-Chinese countries since Chinese churches are sending short-term mission teams to Africa, Europe and Latin America to minister to diaspora Chinese. Therefore, Chinese diaspora cooperation in mission is not merely a theory, but a real practice of Chinese churches in the United States.

Collaboration partners in STM	Frequency
no other people	6
local Chinese Christians from the mission field	134
local non-Chinese Christians from the mission field	39
Chinese Christians from USA	54
non-Chinese Christians from USA	23
Chinese Christians from other countries	22
non-Chinese Christians from other countries	11
Chinese non-Christians	4
Non-Chinese non-Christians	3
Other	5
Total	**301**

Table 4.6. Collaboration Partners in STM

As for partnership, the research data reports that about 37.1 percent of the responding Chinese churches have partnerships with churches in other countries (see table 4.7). This percentage is much lower than the megachurches in the USA: about 84.9 percent of them have partnerships with churches in other countries.[10] Yet my research data also shows that about 70 percent of US Chinese churches have sent at least one short-term mission team to other countries in the past years.[11] This result suggests that most Chinese churches in the USA have not developed partnerships in other countries, although many US Chinese churches may have built up relationships with overseas churches through organizing their own short-term mission trips.

---

10. Priest, Wilson and Johnson, "U.S. Megachurches," 100.
11. For detailed discussion, please see chapter 5.

Partnership	Frequency	Valid Percent
NO	175	62.9
YES	103	37.1
Total	278	100.0

Table 4.7. Partnership among US Chinese Churches

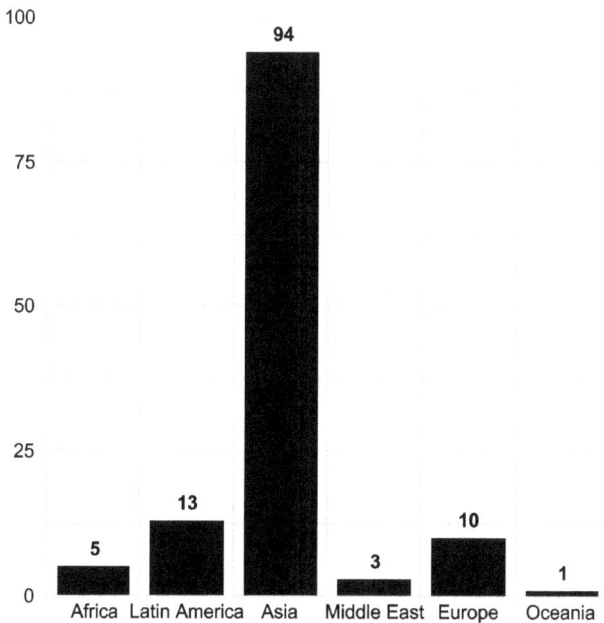

Figure 4.12. Number of Churches Partnering with Churches in the Listed Regions

The data also shows that most Chinese churches in the USA are partnering with churches in Asia (see figure 4.12). Among those churches that have partnerships with churches in Asia, 81 of 91 churches are partnering with churches in the countries or areas with an ethnic Chinese majority, e.g. mainland China, Hong Kong, Singapore and Taiwan. China is the top country where 64 churches have partnerships with Chinese churches in the USA, and the second is Taiwan with 31. Some of the Chinese churches in the USA have partnerships with churches in China and Taiwan at the same time. Thus it suggests a partnership among ethnic Chinese churches is the major kind of partnership for Chinese churches in the United States.

As for the kind of partnership, from those 87 churches which answered this descriptive question, 35 of them say their partnership is "short-term missions & mission cooperation," 28 say "financial support," 20 say "training or theology education" and 4 answer, "sister church." From this data we see that mission cooperation is the main type of partnership among Chinese churches, and this agrees with the other research data we discussed earlier. We need to take note that partnerships as "sister churches" among the same denomination are very few for Chinese churches in the United States. One of the reasons is that most of the Chinese churches in the USA partner with churches in mainland China, and in PRC, Western denominations are not allowed due to their political situation. When I interviewed a Chinese pastor from a Lutheran church in California about the partnership with churches in other countries, he responded, "There is no such thing as denomination in mainland China so we do not need to consider this."

Partnership	No. of churches
STM & mission cooperation	35
Financial support	28
Training or theology education	20
Sister church	4
Total	**87**

Table 4.8. Summary of Partnership

When I interviewed Chinese church leaders, many of them have been either practicing diaspora cooperation in mission or they have this kind of vision. One Chinese pastor from a Christian & Missionary Alliance church in the Midwest explained to me how their church runs short-term mission:

> Since 1998 we had the first person that went on STM. At that time we cooperated with our denomination, which saw the needs in Israel . . . The field director in Israel is American. He saw many Chinese workers were invited by Israelite

government – actually through some brokers – to come to Israel [to] build up houses, which were the housings for the returned diaspora Israelites. That's how we started. So basically we can put it in this way about our way to do STM: We cooperate with our denomination and also "Chinese Churches Association of C&MA in USA," which is formed by all the Chinese C&MA churches in North America . . . I should put it this way, from the East Coast to West Coast of USA. There are about 70 Chinese C&MA churches so they organized an association. And of course this association also belongs to our denomination. This association also conducts lots of ministries of church planting in many different mission fields, and we cooperate with them and join them, or we are invited to cooperate with them. Therefore basically our way of doing STM is: First, we co-work with our denomination and their Chinese Churches Association of C&MA in USA to do STM. According to their needs and expectations, we recruit talented people from our church. Therefore the size of team can vary from 2 persons – because we do not prefer someone going on his own, so at least 2 – to 7 or 8 persons. In the past we also received the needs of STM from non-C&MA groups – not very often but still happened sometimes. So the simplest way we put it is: First, according to the needs of mission field. Of course now we also explore new fields on our own, but from the past more often we do STM according to the mission fields. Second, we cooperate according to these needs, which means, we recruit people with talents accordingly. Third, before we leave for the field, we have intensive trainings for the STM.

This model of running short-term mission as diaspora collaboration is the mission CCCOWE has been advocating. From this C&MA pastor's point of view, the way of doing missions is easier for their church since they just need to follow their denomination's direction and send out teams. A Chinese pastor from the branch of Bread of Life Christian Church put it in this way, "I feel that since the Chinese Christians in USA have higher education, and also people in USA have higher income . . . from these two aspects I always feel we can help best other churches – churches in the mission fields. First, we can train them, and second is we can support them financially. These are the two major directions I have been going." He told me he himself was also involved in the STM of "training or teaching the local ministers the concept of church" in mainland China. A Lutheran pastor in California also told me that their short-term mission teams have worked together with Christians from Hong Kong, and he also invited other churches – both Lutheran and non-Lutheran – to join their ministry in China. His goal is "to mobilize the Chinese churches in North America and Hong Kong to do missions in China together." From this Lutheran pastor's experiences we see multiple transnational ties[12] as the key of their short-term mission. He further explains his vision:

> In 2003 I actually wrote down my vision, which is "global Chinese ministries proposal." Of course I'm thinking [of] the Lutheran church. Because when there are many of our brothers and sisters rising up, and they are bilingual, bi-cultural, and some are tri-lingual . . . If they are sent out, they don't need to spend much money to learn language, and they also know the culture, and so can be the bridge between the locals and mission agency.

In the case of the Chinese C&MA church and Lutheran church, although their denomination can facilitate their overseas mission work or provide some connection, the key is still the trans-state networks, as Sheffer points out in his definition of ethnonational diaspora.

Advantage of Language

Many church leaders mentioned the advantage of languages of Chinese churches when they are doing short-term missions. The Bread of Life Christian Church pastor brought up the idea that Chinese Christians in the USA also have the advantage of fluency in English when doing missions compared with Chinese in Taiwan or China. A Chinese pastor from

---

12. Yang, "Chinese Christian Transnationalism," 133.

a Baptist church shared his experiences of collaborating with a (Caucasian) American church on a short-term mission in China:

> Why is the ministry in L city not well developed? It's because the barrier of languages. They (American STM teams) spoke English (to the local Chinese) and we were the interpreters, we could not talk to the local in Chinese and share the gospel directly in Chinese . . . when they were witnessing in English we translated for them so there were barriers in language.

As a result, that Baptist pastor decided not to invest in this ministry with the American church. They still sent interpreters to join them, but at the same time invested more on their own short-term mission programs in China. He believes that being able to witness to the locals straightforwardly without a language barrier is a better way of doing short-term missions.

As mentioned earlier by different scholars and church leaders, the unity in language is an important factor for Chinese diaspora cooperation in mission. According to my research data, the majority of the Chinese churches in the USA are preaching in Mandarin and English on Sunday, and their Mandarin and English congregations are also generally larger. It could be helpful when they go overseas to minister to their fellow Chinese people. In the questionnaire, when asking, "In the most recent mission trip, what were the first languages of the participants of the short-term mission teams of your church," among those 224 churches that send short-term mission teams, 136 of them answer "Mandarin" and 102 of them answer "English" (see figure 4.13). It should be noted that one short-term mission team can have members who speak different mother tongues, so these answers are multiple.

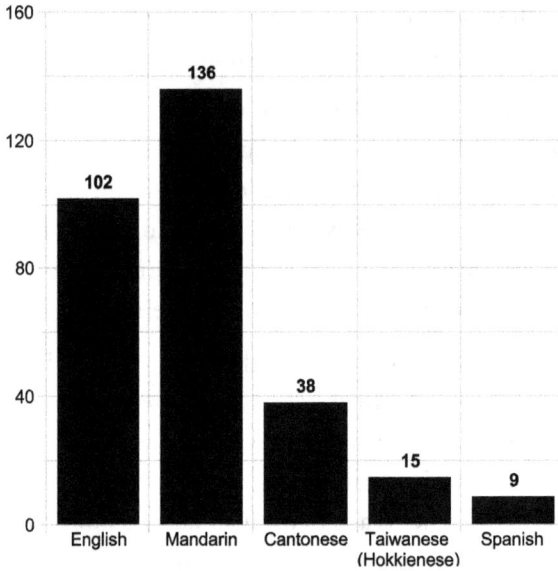

Figure 4.13. Number of Churches Whose STM Team Members Are Speaking These Languages

As for the mother tongue of the local people whom the short-term mission teams are serving, the data reports that out of 224 churches that send short-term mission teams, 141 of them are serving the people whose mother tongue is Mandarin and the other languages are relatively rare (see figure 4.14).

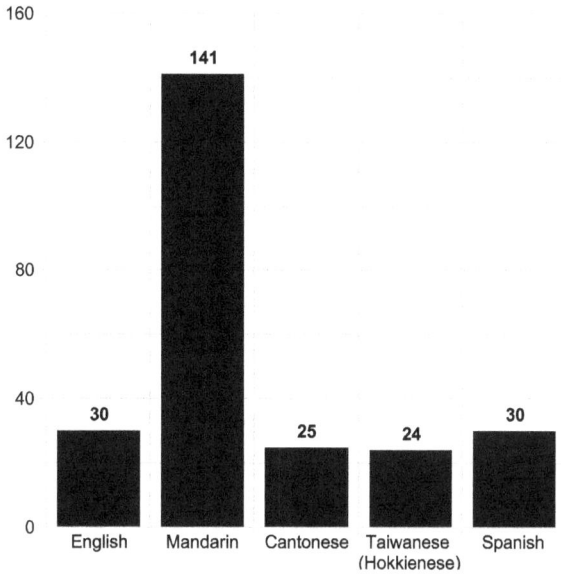

Figure 4.14. Number of Churches Whose STM Teams Are Serving Local People Speaking These Languages

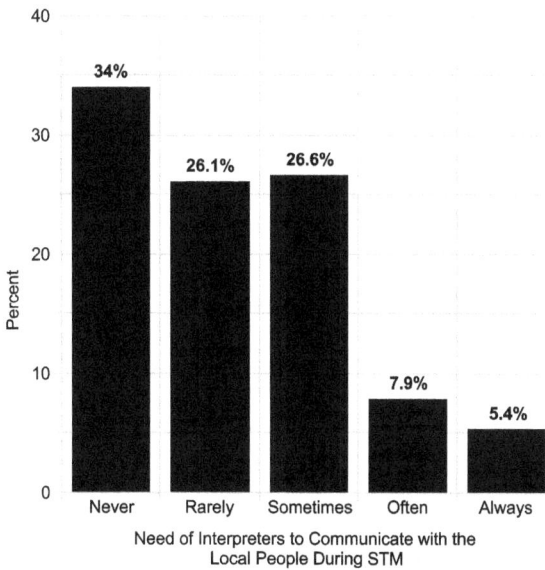

Figure 4.15. Need of Interpreters to Communicate with the Local During STM (N=203)

This data suggests that most Chinese churches are sending short-term mission teams to Mandarin-speaking areas, and most of their team members are Mandarin-speaking as well, which is expected. When asking, "did your short-term mission teams need interpreters to communicate with the local people whom they were serving?" most of churches (60.1%) answer "never" or "rarely" and only 13.3 percent of them answer "often" or "always" (see figure 4.15).

It is not surprising that there is a significant positive correlation between the need for interpreters and the target people in the short-term mission field (r= 0.338, $p < 0.01$), which means that those churches that do not need interpreters during their short-term mission are more likely those who send their STM to minister to Chinese people.

Furthermore, churches that do not need interpreters during short-term missions are more likely to support long-term missionaries serving ethnic Chinese people (r= -0.178, $p < 0.05$). The data also report that there is a correlation between the need of interpreters in STM and the ministry priority of churches. Those churches that see "mission to Chinese" as a higher priority are less likely to need interpreters in the short-term mission field (r= -0.204, $p < 0.01$).

Correlation with "Need of interpreters during STM"	Spearman's rho
How many of these long-term missionaries are serving/ reaching out to ethnic Chinese people?	-0.178*
The primary ministry for the STM teams in these countries/ areas is to non-Chinese	0.388**
"Mission to Chinese" as high priority	-0.204**

Table 4.9. Correlation with "Need of Interpreters during STM" (*Correlation is significant at the 0.05 level; **Correlation is significant at the 0.01 level.)

The research result shows the advantage in language that Chinese diaspora have when they practice "mission through diaspora." As many church leaders point out, without language barriers, it is easier to mobilize their church members to join short-term missions. Furthermore, overseas Chinese Christians read, teach and memorize the same version of the Chinese Bible

– Chinese Union Version – whether they live in mainland China, Taiwan, North America or Europe. Of course, there are several different versions of the Chinese Bible, but for many reasons, most Chinese-speaking Christians favor the Chinese Union Version. Chinese Union Version Bible was translated by Western missionaries and published in China in 1919, and it has been so influential and popular among Chinese in different parts of the world that it just had a minor revision version in 2010.[13] In the articles "Chinese Christian Transnationalism: Diverse Networks of a Houston Church," Fenggang Yang also notices that the Chinese Christian publications are mostly from Asia (Hong Kong and Taiwan) to North America, including the hymnal books.[14] In fact, not only the Bible and Chinese Christian books, even Chinese worship music is transnational. When I was serving in the Chinese churches in China, Germany and the USA, I discovered that they were all familiar with the same Chinese worship songs. These songs are composed by Chinese composers or groups in Taiwan, the USA and China, and the lyrics are in Mandarin. All of these elements are very helpful and convenient for Chinese diaspora when they share the gospel among Chinese immigrants and serve alongside other Chinese Christians from different countries.

A Progressional Mission Approach

When I interviewed the leaders of Chinese churches, I could see their missiologies all at some level share the idea of "in Jerusalem, Judaea, Samaria and to the ends of the earth." When asking why most Chinese churches in the USA invest most resources in outreach and serving ethnic Chinese, they answer in these three directions: (1) the biblical model in the book of Acts, which is further developed to "E1, E2, E3 theory" or "same culture, near culture and different culture" idea, (2) entrust the cross-cultural mission to the second generation, the so-called "ABC" (American-Born Chinese), (3) the American culture influence – pursuing security and comfort, or the

---

13. It is also noteworthy that even the revision of Chinese Union Version is a transnational task: a collaboration of Chinese Bible scholars from mainland China, Hong Kong, Taiwan, Malaysia, Singapore, Australia and America. C.f. the website of Hong Kong Bible Society: http://www.hkbs.org.hk/tw/content/10-about-6 (accessed 15 April 2014).

14. Yang, "Chinese Christian Transnationalism," 136.

Chinese-culture influence – reserved and being self-contained. Here I will elaborate more on the first and second direction on this topic. To better understand these informants' idea, we will review the E1, E2 and E3 theory and the biblical model in the book of Acts first.

In the article, "The New Macedonia: A Revolutionary New Era in Mission Begins," Ralph Winter introduces the idea of different levels of evangelism – E-1, E-2, E-3,[15] and this idea is developed from the Great Commission, "and you will be my witnesses in Jerusalem, and in all Judea and Samaria, and to the ends of the earth" (Acts 1:8). For the disciples in Jerusalem, sharing the gospel with Jews in Jerusalem and Judea was E-1 evangelism, with Samaritans is E-2 evangelism, and to the ends of the earth is E-3 evangelism.

Take Paul as an example. He was Jewish diaspora born in Tarsus (Acts 22:3) and fluent in both Greek and Aramaic, and thus evangelizing the Greek-speaking Gentiles was for him not E-3 but E-2. In this sense, he was the best person to be an instrument to preach the gospel before the Gentiles and their kings. In the first century, 7 percent of the population in the Roman Empire was Jewish,[16] which means there were a great number of Jews scattered throughout the Roman Empire. As a result, "it is beyond doubt that in the Diaspora, Jewish relations with the surrounding Gentile world were much closer than in Palestine."[17] Therefore, it was very convenient for Paul to travel around the Roman Empire and preach the gospel among the Jewish Diaspora and Gentiles. We see how God used all these events to fulfill his will. He used (1) political power, for example a united empire and citizenship (i.e. Roman citizenship of Paul) (Acts 22:27-28), and (2) human authorities (i.e. Caesar).

With this kind of missiology in their minds, when I was interviewing the Chinese church leaders, I could see they are following this model when they are explaining their goal and visions of missions. The mission model of the apostle Paul has a strong influence on Chinese Christians, as the Baptist

---

15. Winter and Hawthorne, *World Christian Movement*.

16. Stephen Neill, *A History of Christian Missions*. 2nd ed. (New York, NY: Penguin Books, 1991), 25.

17. Irina Levinskaya, *The Book of Acts in its Diaspora Setting*, *The Book of Acts in Its First Century Setting*, vol. 5 (Grand Rapids, MI: Eerdmans, 1996), 12.

pastor suggested. When asking the possible reason that Chinese Christians are mostly doing outreach to Chinese, he said the first thought came into his mind is "when Paul went out to share the gospel, he always preached in the Jewish synagogue first." The Baptist pastor in Texas put it in this way:

> If you want the mission mobilization to be successful, the congregation has to feel they have the same burden. For example, if in the first year we said, "Let us to go to Africa!" But they have never been to Africa, and they may not feel connected to the black people. Then you want to send them, maybe at most only one or two will be very interested. But if it's Chinese, their hometown is either China or Taiwan or from other places where Chinese people live . . . if they can return to their hometown, they will feel much more connected. This is the first step. But every church needs to ask this question, "When will we move forward to E-2, E-3 from E-0, E-1?" For example, this March we went to Israel for tourism, and we saved 3 days to join some (ministries). It's also for some Chinese workers there. So we still are doing E-2. But last year when we went to Thailand, it's totally E-3, because we were with a minority people group . . . We have to challenge them, challenge them, "when and who can do completely cross-cultural, completely E-3 ministry?" (Chinese Baptist pastor in Texas)

He further explained, in terms of ratio, there would be always fewer people willing to do E-3 missions compared to E-1 or E-2, but it is fine. He believed that we do not have to have many people do E-3, but those people who are doing E-3 can be a bridge of culture and language, and mobilize more local people to take over the ministry.

Another viewpoint often mentioned by these church leaders is to develop and train the second-generation Chinese Americans to do cross-cultural missions. I have also heard this idea spoken by pastors from different overseas Chinese churches. The main reason they support this idea is that they believe the second generation can master the English language better than their parents, and they grow up in a bi-cultural environment, which is also preparing them to do ministry cross-culturally. An elder from a

Chinese church on the East Coast believes that second-generation Chinese
Americans are the key to mobilizing cross-cultural missions:

> In Chinese churches there is so-called English congregation,
> which is still not the main congregation, because the church
> starts with Chinese people! For us, in fact our English con-
> gregation is slowly getting strong. Now speaking of the ratio,
> for example – no matter in deacon board or elder board – the
> ratio of the members was 90:10 in the past, but now it im-
> proved to 70:30. And of course we hope they can enter the
> so-called "decision-making circle," and then they will be more
> active to join the cross-cultural missions. . . . If you want to
> mobilize mission – especially in Chinese church – you should
> always start from Chinese people. You need to educate them
> on the concept of missions, or educate the whole church, and
> then they will slowly notice the importance of cross-cultural
> missions. If you even didn't do or rarely do the same-cultural
> ministry, you don't even need to talk about cross-cultural mis-
> sion. (Chinese elder in the East Coast)

When examining this idea carefully, we find this also agrees with the
concept of "first E-1, then E-2 and E-3," (i.e. the first generation does
mostly E-1 and E-2, and then the second generation can undertake E-3).
The apostle Paul even can be the model missionary for the second-generation diaspora Chinese. The above elder's church actually has fairly well-
developed short-term mission programs and has been very involved in
cross-cultural missions in Latin America and Central Asia compared with
the average Chinese churches in the United States. Their model may be
adopted by other Chinese churches in United States.

Both this elder and the Baptist pastor bring up a progressional way of
doing missions in the Chinese context – from same culture, to near culture
to different culture. From the research data, we can also see that most of
Chinese churches in the USA are still in the stage of doing missions in the
"same culture" or "near culture."

The quantitative research data also implies that this kind of progressional missiology is embraced by Chinese diaspora. When I tried to find
the correlation between different ministry priorities and mission activities,

I found that there is no correlation between "mission to Chinese" and mission activities such as frequency of short-term mission and mission conference, number of long-term missionaries supported by churches, and the percentage of money spent on overseas ministry (see table 4.10). It means churches that have high priority on "missions to Chinese" are not supporting more long-term missionaries, sending STM teams more often, holding mission conferences more often and spending a higher percentage on overseas ministry. Although "missions to Chinese" is the top priority of most Chinese churches in the states, ironically it does not seem to make churches more (or less) involved in missions.

Correlation with prioritized ministry as "missions to Chinese"	Spearman's rho
Frequency of sending STM teams	0.003
Frequency of holding mission conference	0.046
Number of long-term missionaries supported by church	-0.112
Percent of money spent on overseas ministries	0.044

Table 4.10. Correlation with Prioritized Ministry as "Missions to Chinese"

But what about the correlations with "mission to the Unreached," which is the second priority of many Chinese churches? It has a significant correlation with the percentage of money spent on overseas ministry, number of long-term missionaries supported by the church and especially on percentage of money spent on overseas ministries, but no correlation with "frequency of sending STM teams" is reported (see table 4.11).

Correlation with prioritized ministry as "Missions to the unreached"	Spearman's rho
Frequency of sending STM teams	0.092
Frequency of holding mission conference	0.126*
Number of long-term missionaries supported by church	0.152*
Percent of money spent on overseas ministries	0.212**

*Table 4.11. Correlation with Prioritized Ministry as "Missions to the Unreached" (*Correlation is significant at the 0.05 level; **Correlation is significant at the 0.01 level.)*

Surprisingly, the ministry priority which has the most significant correlation with mission activities of Chinese churches in the USA is "Evangelizing Muslims" (see table 4.12). It means churches that see evangelizing Muslims as a high priority are more likely to send STM teams and hold mission conferences more frequently, support more long-term missionaries overseas, and spend a higher percentage on overseas ministries.

Correlation with prioritized ministry as "Evangelizing Muslims"	Spearman's rho
Frequency of sending STM teams	0.221**
Frequency of holding mission conference	0.214**
Number of long-term missionaries supported by church	0.358**
Percent of money spent on overseas ministries	0.235**

*Table 4.12. Correlation with Prioritized Ministry as "Evangelizing Muslims" (**Correlation is significant at the 0.01 level.)*

According to the survey, only about 20 percent of Chinese churches in the USA report evangelizing Muslims as their top or secondary priority as a ministry concern, and yet these churches are likely those more active in missions. This implies that those Chinese churches that already move forward from "E-2" to "E-3" or "near culture" to "different culture" are more developed in their mission programs. Although there is a significant correlation, it is hard to make a judgment about the cause and effect. We do not know if it is because these churches have had better-developed mission programs that they started to be concerned more about evangelizing Muslims, or if it is the other way around. But at least this data shows that it is not missions to Chinese, but missions to Muslims, which is the prioritized concerned of a more mission-minded Chinese church in United States.

Summary

From previous studies, we see many Chinese church leaders, mission organization leaders and Chinese scholars suggest that in this century overseas Chinese Christians have the advantages of practicing mission work similar to the Jewish diaspora in the first century. Both the qualitative and quantitative data shows that the transnational networks of US Chinese churches have opened the door for them to do ministries and go for mission trips to mainland China, Hong Kong and Taiwan, and even non-Chinese countries in Europe, Latin America and Africa. Transnationalism has existed in overseas Chinese economies, and now it can be applied to overseas Chinese missions.

From the research data, we can see the "E-2 model" of mission among diaspora has been utilized well by Chinese Christians in the USA as "mission through diaspora." Although it is not an exact parallel with the Jews scattered in the Roman Empire, since the Jews had been already part of the Roman Empire, there are many similarities between Chinese diaspora in the era of globalization and Jewish diaspora in the first century, as discussed in the previous chapter. There are about 71 million Chinese immigrants and migrants in the world[18] and from the previous data we can say Chinese are just about everywhere, even in the areas where people strongly resist the gospel like the Middle East and South Asia. According to the data of CCCOWE in 2011, there are about 0.26 million Chinese people living in Middle East.[19] Although some of the Chinese-speaking people are not residents but businessmen, there are still benefits to cooperate with these local Chinese Christians because they are familiar with the culture

18. CCCOWE, "The Statistics Data."

19. See https://www.cccowe.org for the sources of the Overseas Chinese population data of CCCOWE.

and already have contacts with the nationals already. These local coworkers should be trained before undertaking mission work. After interviewing
Chinese church leaders in DC area, Yang summarizes the Chinese way of
thinking for global Christian missions:

> Chinese have spread to many countries of all continents
> around the world, and Chinese continue to leave China in
> large numbers. Chinese Christian leaders claim that if every-
> thing is under the control of God, the spread of Chinese peo-
> ple must have the purpose of God. For evangelical Christians,
> this purpose could not be anything else but to spread the gos-
> pel to all peoples of the world. They believe that diasporic
> Chinese not only occupy strategic geographic positions, but
> they also have a great advantage over European and American
> missionaries.[20]

Although the Chinese way of thinking and doing mission may seem
to be a little optimistic, from this research we can see that most Chinese
churches in the USA are actually taking action – they support missionaries, hold mission conferences and send out short-term mission teams.
Moreover, the church leaders themselves are also involved in mission trips,
even though their churches do not have mission pastors. All the Chinese
church leaders whom I interviewed recognized the fact that Chinese
churches in the USA have invested most of their resources on ministries
to Chinese, but this is understandable since Chinese people make up one-
fifth of the world's population and American Chinese Christians have the
advantage of language, culture and transnational networks. Yet at the same
time they generally agreed that Chinese churches have to undertake cross-
cultural missions as a goal for the near future, and they are in the process of
moving forward to that goal.

In sum, mission through diaspora and diaspora cooperation in mission
fits well in the Chinese context because these kinds of transnational networks and paradigms have existed among Chinese diaspora for centuries.
Diaspora Chinese traders have been known for their ability for building
up connections and utilizing transnational resources to make profits. They

---

20. Yang, *Chinese Christians in America*, 174.

look for business opportunities and are very practical and realistic about their investments – they want to create the most benefits in the most efficient way. Through this research we see similar patterns in the way diaspora Chinese carry out their missions: they start with near and convenient mission – reach out to the Chinese in their community, and then move on to minister to Chinese in other places through sending short-term mission teams. They look for ministry opportunities and use all kinds of transnational networks to make connections. Like overseas Chinese capitalists having advantages of culture, language and connection in doing business in mainland China, overseas Chinese Christians also have more mission opportunities and efficient ministries there for the same reason. The difference may be that overseas Chinese investments are welcomed by the PRC government, yet overseas Chinese mission work in mainland China technically is still against the law.

We have examined the general missions activities of the US Chinese church. Next, we turn to their short-term mission practice, which also bears distinctive traits that distinguish it from the short-term mission practice of other churches in the United States.

CHAPTER 5

Findings on Short-Term Missions by Chinese Churches in the USA

In the last decade, the American the short-term mission movement has been studied by missiologists, anthropologists and sociologists, generating many articles and books on this topic. Nearly all studies on short-term mission focus on the movement in North America, regardless of the fact that Asian, African and Latino churches also send out short-term mission teams while also receiving short-term mission teams. Furthermore, the intra-ethnic cooperation of the diaspora church in North America is also remarkable. Some ethnic groups, such as Korean and Chinese in North America, have been connecting with or ministering to their kinsmen in their homeland or other countries through short-term mission.[1] For example, my Korean American friend went on a short-term mission with other Korean Americans from their ethnic Korean church to North Korea for a medical short-term mission. Born and raised in Taiwan, I was also involved in Chinese diaspora ministries, working with Chinese Christians in North America to reach out to Chinese in Germany. The Chinese church in the Chicago suburbs where I regularly worship sends short-term mission teams every summer to China.

Chin T. Wang's idea of "transnational resources" is very relevant in this kind of mission today.[2] Transnational communities are common in Chinese society. Many overseas Chinese are scattered throughout Southeast Asia and

---

1. Priest, "Short-Term Mission," 95.

2. Chin T. (John) Wang, "Urban Church Resources for Short-Term Mission," in *Effective Engagement in Short-Term Missions: Doing It Right!*, ed. Robert Priest (Pasadena, CA: William Carey Library, 2008), 248.

North America in the pursuit of economic, political and cultural interests, and they still live in a Chinese community and speak Chinese languages for generations. Thus they feel more motivation and less difficulty to do mission to their own people. This research mainly focuses on this kind of collaboration of diaspora with their ethnic kinsmen in short-term mission.

In the previous chapter, we saw how Chinese churches in the USA practice "mission through diaspora," and how "short-term missions as transnationalism" plays a significant role in this kind of practice. The research data shows how short-term missions connect the national Chinese and overseas Chinese, or Chinese diaspora, from different parts of the world through collaboration in missions and partnership. This chapter focuses on short-term missions and shows how Chinese churches in the USA do short-term missions, followed by a brief evaluation of its strengths and growth areas.

Information Discovered from This Research

When analyzing the web pages of Chinese churches in USA, I found that many churches (more than 50) put their short-term mission programs on their websites. They upload the pictures of previous short-term missions and/or make announcements about their upcoming trips on their websites. From these websites, it seems that Chinese churches in the USA are very active in short-term missions. But to know the real situation requires careful study.

According to the survey, out of the 316 responding churches, there are about 27.5 percent of Chinese churches in the USA that say they never send out short-term mission teams, and more than half (51.6%) of them have had one or more short-term mission trips every year (see figure 5.1). If we look at the correlation, the data shows that there is a significant correlation between the frequency of sending STM teams and frequency of holding mission conferences, church size, number of long-term missionaries supported, and percentage of budget on overseas ministries (see table 5.1). From chapter 4 we already know there is a positive correlation between church size, the number of missionaries supported, and percentage of money spent on overseas ministries, and these three all have significant positive correlations with frequency of sending STM teams. This data suggests this kind of Chinese church in the USA is more likely to send STM teams more frequently: larger in size, supporting more overseas long-term missionaries, higher percentage spent on overseas ministry, and holding mission conference more frequently.

Correlation with "frequency of sending STM teams"	Spearman's rho
How often does the church hold mission conferences?	0.375**
The approximate regular attendance of a normal weekend (including adults and children)	0.551**
The approximate number of overseas long-term missionaries supported by church	0.401**
The percentage of money spent on overseas ministries	0.275**

*Table 5.1. Correlation with "Frequency of Sending STM Teams" (**Correlation is significant at the 0.01 level.)*

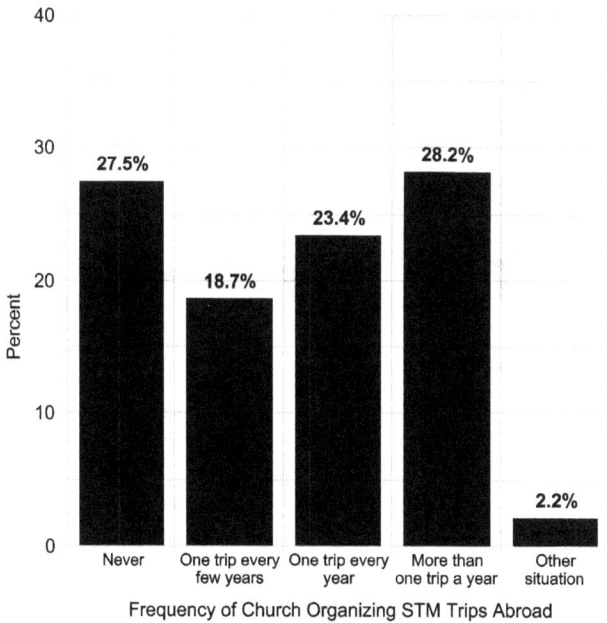

Figure 5.1. Frequency of Church Organizing Overseas STM trips (N=316)

If we look at the number of people from Chinese churches in the USA who have traveled overseas for short-term missions in 2012, it shows almost 60 percent of Chinese churches in the USA sent church members for overseas short-term mission trips in 2012, and about half of them (46.2%) have sent one to twenty people overseas for short-term missions in 2012 (see figure 5.2). The survey data also reports that 5.1 percent of the regular attendees (adults and children) of Chinese churches in the USA went on a mission trip in 2012.

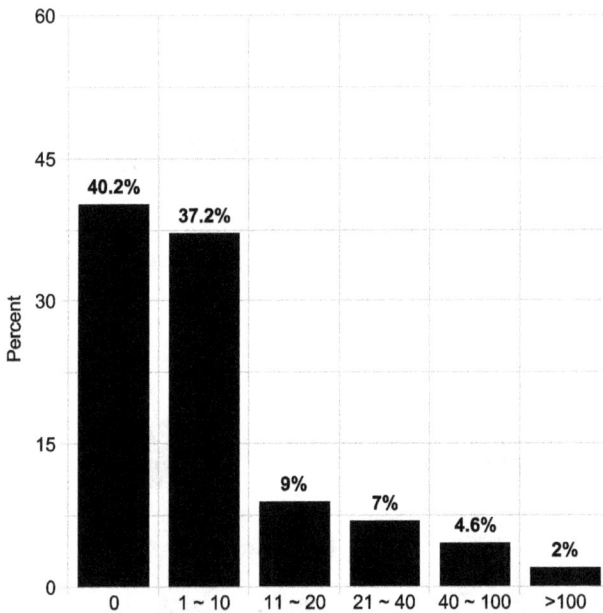

Figure 5.2. Number of Persons Traveling Overseas for STM in 2012 (N=301)

When comparing this data with US megachurches and Korean American churches, it is interesting to see that the number of people in Chinese churches going on an overseas STM is similar with Korean churches in the United States. Half of US Korean churches (52.2%) also sent out one to twenty people for short-term missions in 2009 (see table 5.2), according to Hong's report. But a higher percentage of Chinese churches sent more than twenty people in a particular year. Considering church size, only about 17 percent of Korean churches in the USA have more than 250 weekly attendees,[3] while about 27 percent of Chinese churches have more than 250 (see chapter 4). As for the average number of attendees (mean), US Korean churches' is 201.5,[4] and US Chinese churches' is 247.9 (see chapter 4). This data suggests that Korean churches are smaller than Chinese churches in size.

Hong also reports that 4.5 percent of the regular attendees of US Korean churches went for overseas short-term mission trips in a year.[5] As for USA megachurches, since most of them are between 2,000–5,000 in size, it is not surprising that most megachurches sent 21–150 persons on an overseas STM in a year.[6] But when considering the percentage of regular attendees of USA megachurches that went on a mission trip, the previous study reports only 3.7 percent in average (mean),[7] which is lower than both Chinese (5.1%) and Korean (4.5%) churches in the USA. This result suggests that even though much smaller in size, ethnic churches like Chinese and Korean churches in the USA are as much involved in short-term missions – if not more involved – as USA megachurches.

No. of STM participants	Percent
0	37.5
1 – 10	40.6
11 – 20	11.6
21 – 40	5.6
>40	4.8

Table 5.2. Number of STM Participants of US Korean Churches in 2009 (N=599)[8]

When asking, "How many teams did your church send for overseas short-term mission trips in 2012?" the data shows that these 297 Chinese churches sent a total of 469 STM teams in 2012. Calculated with the data

---

3. Hong, "Interracial and Interethnic Attitudes," 67.

4. Ibid., 68.

5. Ibid., 69.

6. Priest, Wilson and Johnson, "U.S. Megachurches," 97.

7. Ibid., 98.

8. Data reported by Hong, "Interracial and Interethnic Attitudes."

of STM participants in 2012, it is roughly eight people for each STM team of Chinese churches in the USA. Of the responding churches, 26.6 percent sent one team, and about 32.6 percent of them sent more than one team. More than half of Chinese churches sent out one to four short-term mission teams in 2012. In total, 59.2 percent of Chinese churches in the USA have sent at least one STM team in 2012 (see figure 5.3).

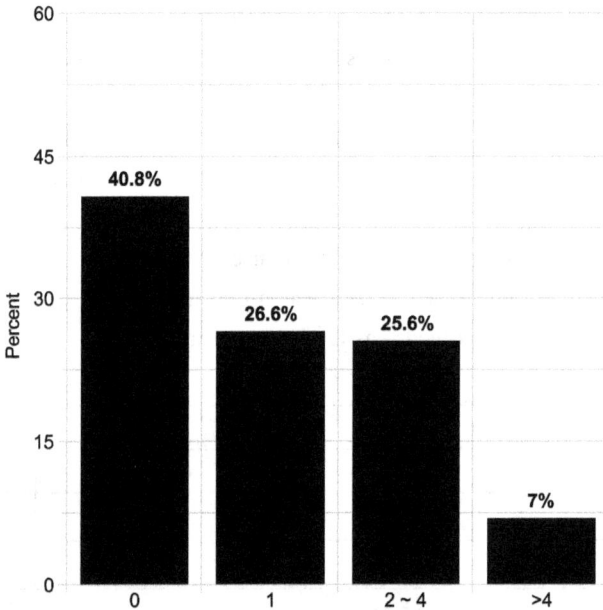

Figure 5.3. Number of STM Teams Sent in 2012 (N=297)

The survey data shows that the majority (68.3%) of short-term mission teams of Chinese churches in the USA spent about seven to fourteen days in the mission field for their most recent trip (see figure 5.4), the mean (average) being 15.1 days and the median 10 days. This result is similar to the data of Korean American churches: 69.3 percent of them spent seven to fourteen days,[9] and previous short-term mission studies also report similar

---

9. Hong, *Interracial and Interethnic Attitudes*, 74.

results.[10] It shows that the general definition of "short-term" – one or two weeks – also applies to Chinese diaspora's short-term mission. Now we have a basic idea of what the short-term mission movement of Chinese American churches look like. In the next section we will look more specifically on where the STM teams go, what they do, who has gone, and whether or not the trips are effective.

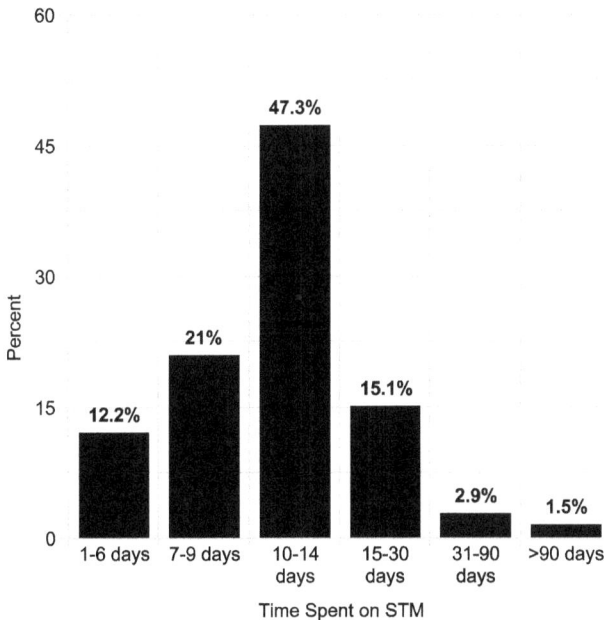

Figure 5.4. Time Spent on STM for Most Recent Trip (N=205)

Where Are the STM Teams Going?

In the last chapter, the transnationalism of Chinese short-term mission was shown by the places where the Chinese churches in the USA sent their short-term mission teams: the data reports that 74.4 percent of US Chinese churches have sent at least one STM team to the areas with an ethnic Chinese majority in 2012, with China as the top destination. Here

10. Priest et al., "Researching"; Kyeong-Sook Park, "Researching Short-Term Missions and Paternalism," in *Effective Engagement in Short-Term Missions: Doing It Right!*, ed. Robert Priest (Pasadena, CA: William Carey Library, 2008).

we provide further analysis on this data and comparison with previous research results. According to survey data, the top eleven destinations of the short-term mission trips by Chinese churches in the USA are China, Taiwan, Mexico, Hong Kong, UK, Germany, Brazil, Thailand, India, Myanmar and Cambodia. Compared with the destinations of US mega-churches[11] and US Korean churches,[12] it is a different kind of list. There are no African countries in the top eleven destinations of Chinese churches in the USA, which is similar to Korean churches. Furthermore, there are only two Latin American countries (Mexico and Brazil) in Chinese churches' top eleven, which are also the only two destinations which overlap with US megachurches. Compared with Chinese churches, both US megachurches and Korean American churches seem to be more Latin American focused on their STM. In addition, there are two European countries in the list of Chinese churches, which are not in Korean and US megachurches' top ten at all (see table 5.3).

US Korean churches STM destinations	US megachurches STM destinations	US Chinese churches STM destinations	US tourists destinations
Mexico	Mexico	China	UK
China	Guatemala	Taiwan	Italy
Dominican	Honduras	Mexico	Spain
Republic	Dominican	Hong Kong	France
Nicaragua	Republic	UK	China
Korea	Nicaragua	Germany	Australia
Thailand	Brazil	Brazil	Mexico
Philippines	South Africa	Thailand	Germany
Peru	Kenya	India	Ireland
Haiti	Uganda	Myanmar	Costa Rica
Guatemala	Haiti		

Table 5.3. Comparison of STM Destinations among Different Churches

---

11. Priest, Wilson, and Johnson, "New Patterns," 98.

12. Hong, *Interracial and Interethnic Attitudes*, 84.

If we compare Chinese churches' top ten destinations with the USA tourists' top ten destinations,[13] we will find more similarities than with the US megachurches' top ten (see table 5.3). This may be the reason that in my survey of US Chinese churches a few respondents mentioned "misunderstanding it as tourism" when talking about the negative side of STM.

This data suggests that the destinations of STM for Chinese churches are not affected by how far the country is, which is different from US megachurches.[14] But if we break down the data to see Chinese churches in different regions of the USA, we still can see the impact of geographical location within the USA on their STM destinations. A higher percentage of Chinese churches on the West Coast sent STM teams to Asia than Chinese churches in other regions, while the churches in the East Coast have the lowest percentage (see table 5.4).

Regions	No. of churches	STM destinations in Asia	Percent
East Coast	96	36	37.5%
Midwest	55	25	45.5%
South	47	24	51.1%
West Coast	114	63	55.3%

Table 5.4. STM Destinations in Asia for Chinese Churches in Different Parts of the USA

13. Priest, Wilson, and Johnson, "New Patterns," 98.
14. Ibid., 99.

US Chinese churches STM destinations	Rank of GDP (PPP) per capita	Rank of GDP (nominal) per capita	Rank of GDP (nominal)
China	93	87	2
Taiwan	18	38	27
Mexico	67	65	14
Hong Kong	7	25	38
UK	21	23	6
Germany	17	21	4
Brazil	81	60	7
Thailand	92	94	32
India	133	138	10
Myanmar	162	154	72
USA	6	10	1

Table 5.5. GDP Data of STM Destinations from International Monetary Fund (2012)

Is there an economic difference in the destinations of the STM by Chinese churches? Although the USA is still the most powerful economy in the world, and previous research shows that Chinese immigrants in the USA generally have high socioeconomic status,[15] Taiwan, Hong Kong, UK and Germany are also well off economically. The overseas Chinese economies have been researched and discussed broadly since the rapid economic growth of Hong Kong, Singapore and Taiwan.[16] China is a more complicated case because it has experienced a fast economic development since the economic "Reform and Opening Up," and has claimed to be the second largest economy in the world,[17] while there is still a very large gap between the cities and villages. The major cities (most of them are near the East Coast) are very well developed, like Shanghai, Guangzhou, Beijing, Tianjin, etc., while places in the remote areas are like different worlds.[18] The interview information does show that Chinese churches are sending STM teams to both well-developed major cities and remote areas. If we use

15. Fan, "Chinese Americans."
16. Tong, *Entrepreneurs*, 148.
17. Hamlin and Li, "China Overtakes Japan."
18. Cao, *Constructing China's Jerusalem*, 126–162.

GDP at purchasing power parity per capita to measure the wealth, according to the data from the International Monetary Fund in 2012, the USA is #6, Taiwan #18, Hong Kong #7, UK #21 and Germany #17, which all lead in the list; while Thailand, China, India and Myanmar are behind (see table 5.5). Since four of the ten STM destinations are considered economically strong according to their GDP at purchasing power parity per capita, we cannot make a strong case on the economic differences for Chinese churches' STMs, though it may still apply to the other destinations.

Since "missions to the unreached" is another high priority for many Chinese churches besides "missions to Chinese," do Chinese churches in the USA send STMs to reach the unreached? We borrow the category of World A (the un-evangelized world), World B (the evangelized non-Christian world) and World C (the Christian world) created by Barrett and Johnson,[19] and find four countries (Mexico, UK, Germany and Brazil) of the top eleven destinations are World C, six are World B and one (Cambodia) is World A. This result shows that "reaching the least reached" is not the main concern when choosing STM destinations for Chinese churches in the USA, though compared with USA megachurches and Korean American churches, Chinese churches did send more STM teams to World B than World C.

We must also pay attention to the fact that there are large Chinese populations in these World B destinations. When considering the Chinese population in these destinations, this top eleven list makes more sense. All the top eleven destinations, except Mexico, have large Chinese populations (more than 100,000), and Chinese churches are already present in all of these top eleven destinations (see table 5.6). In chapter 4, we saw that the data shows that Chinese churches in the USA did send STM teams to Europe, Latin America, and Africa to minister to Chinese diaspora. The data also shows that they often collaborate with ethnic Chinese of other countries in their short-term missions. The choices of STM destinations reflect this kind of mission practice. According to the research results regarding the top priority of most Chinese churches in the USA, "missions to Chinese" may affect the STM destination choices more than "missions to

---

19. Barrett and Johnson, *World Christian Trends*, 912.

the unreached." In sum, these comparisons of data with previous research show that the destinations of STM by Chinese churches in the USA are not as much affected by distance and economic difference as USA megachurches and Korean American churches. As we discussed in chapter 4, "missions to Chinese" as the ministry priority and the "Chinese first" principle are the main influence.

Top 11 STM destinations	Ethnic Chinese population in STM destinations	No. of Chinese churches
China	1,347,000,000	No official data[21]
Taiwan	23,142,000	3,728
Mexico	25,000	2
Hong Kong	7,061,000	1,250
UK	335,000	103
Germany	110,000	25
Brazil	224,000	38
Thailand	7,178,000	20
India	155,000	2
Myanmar	1,090,000	57
Cambodia	350,000	9

Table 5.6. Population and Church Data from CCCOWE, 2011[20]

When I interviewed the Chinese pastor from an independent church in Illinois, he explained to me how they chose the places to send STM teams: "First, the missionaries or mission agencies have needs, and they contact our church or brothers and sisters of our church, so they decide to go. Second, our church initiates to go. It means that we have some missionaries, and we contact them, and ask them if they would like us to go."

---

20. CCCOWE published their data of Overseas Chinese churches on the quarterly journal *Chinese Church Today* in 2011, where they explained that they collected these data of Chinese churches through their local branches around the world, and also used the local directories of Chinese churches produced by Chinese Christian Herald Crusades.

21. According to the 2009 data provided by the Chinese government, there were 58,000 Protestant churches in China (see Yang, *Religion in China*, 94) but this only includes the registered Three-Self churches. There are also house churches which are not government-approved and their number has been growing (Ibid., 107–108).

Other church leaders all mentioned that their STMs started with some kind of relationship or networking, so-called "*guanxi*" in Chinese. Usually it is someone they know on the mission field or in charge of the ministry and create the platform for them to bring in STM teams. The most common case is that the church has been supporting missionaries or ministries there, and the missionaries invite their STM teams to come to support their ministry. The data also shows most churches are also sending STM teams to the destinations where they have long-term missionaries (see table 5.7). This may also explain the significant positive correlation between the number of long-term missionaries supported by church and the frequency of sending STM teams (see table 5.1). All these above show that transnational ties are the key to short-term mission in the Chinese context.

Top 11 long-term missionaries' fields	Top 11 STM destinations
China	China
Taiwan	Taiwan
Thailand	Mexico
Hong Kong	Hong Kong
Brazil	UK
UK	Germany
Germany	Brazil
India	Thailand
Philippines	India
Kyrgyzstan	Myanmar
Myanmar	Cambodia

Table 5.7. Long-Term Mission and Short-Term Mission Destinations

The survey data also shows that almost 60 percent of the Chinese churches that have sent STM teams always or often return to the same mission field repeatedly (see figure 5.5). When I was interviewing church leaders, most of them expressed their points of view on deciding whether to go to the same mission field or not. Some of them tried to find a balance between "maintain the partnership and complete their tasks" and "explore new fields and give church members new challenges." The Lutheran pastor put it this way, "we almost go to the same place every year because we only

have two or three weeks; if we go to different places every year, then every-
one will feel it is like tourism." In the past six years, his church has focused
on only three locations in China. But later he also mentioned last year they
sent their first STM team to Thailand, to give them a new experience and
prepare them to do a little bit of "E-3" ministry.

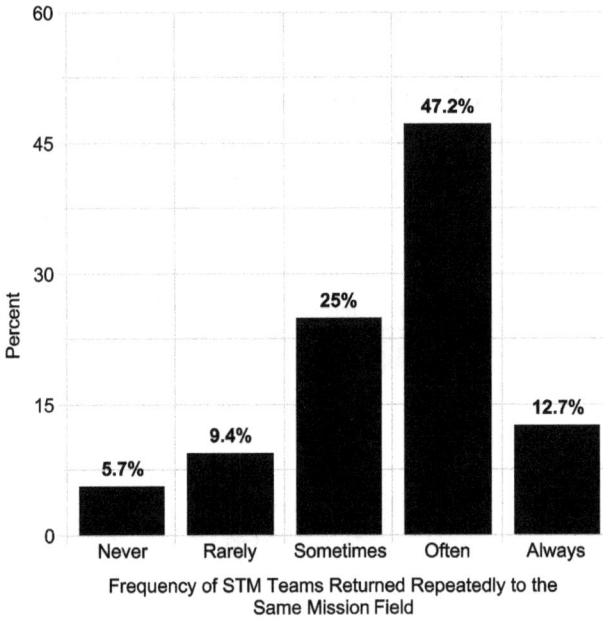

Figure 5.5. Frequency of STM Returned to the Same Field (N= 212)

The pastor of the independent church in Illinois told me there were two
different views on STM which have been debated in his church: one is that
STM is for the people in the mission field; the other view is that STM is
for their own church members' missions training/education and spiritual
growth. If STM is for the local people in the mission field, then they would
"hope the contribution of the STM can focus more on one place." But if
STM is for their church members, he said, "it does not really matter where
the mission field is. The most important thing is what STM brings to the
development of our brothers and sisters." From the statistic data of this
research, most of the Chinese churches returned to the same mission field

repeatedly, which suggests most Chinese churches in the USA may incline more toward the first view.

What Are Their Tasks?

In chapter 4, the survey data showed that about 60 percent of Chinese churches in the USA did not need or rarely needed interpreters in their recent overseas STM trips, and 69 percent of Chinese churches in the USA sent their overseas STM teams to minister to ethnic Chinese in 2012. So in the previous section we learned that the Chinese churches in the USA most often send their STM teams to countries with a larger Chinese population to minister to national Chinese or Chinese diaspora, which shows their prioritized ministry concern: "missions to Chinese." With less language and cultural barriers, what kind of ministry activities do their STM teams focus on?

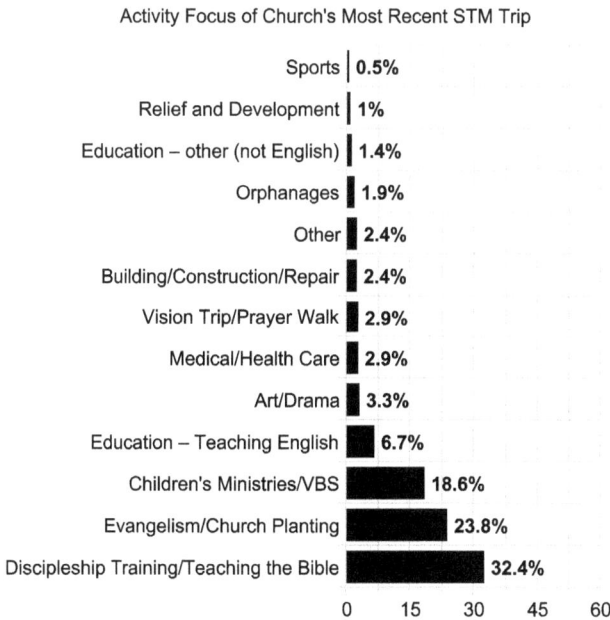

Activity Focus of Church's Most Recent STM Trip

Activity	Percentage
Sports	0.5%
Relief and Development	1%
Education – other (not English)	1.4%
Orphanages	1.9%
Other	2.4%
Building/Construction/Repair	2.4%
Vision Trip/Prayer Walk	2.9%
Medical/Health Care	2.9%
Art/Drama	3.3%
Education – Teaching English	6.7%
Children's Ministries/VBS	18.6%
Evangelism/Church Planting	23.8%
Discipleship Training/Teaching the Bible	32.4%

Figure 5.6. STM Activities (N=210)

Based on my observation and personal experiences of STM by Chinese American churches, most send their STM teams to teach and equip the

local Chinese Christians. They usually offer intense Bible study or training courses during the time they stay. Thus, in the survey questions on the
activity focus of STM, I indicated "Discipleship training/Bible teaching" as
a choice, and the survey data shows that this is the top activity focus of the
STM teams sent by Chinese churches in the USA (see figure 5.6).

	US Korean churches	US megachurches
Top focus	Evangelism, Church Planting	Building, Construction, Repair
	VBS, Children's Ministries.	Evangelism, Church Planting
	Medical, health care	VBS, Children's ministries
	Building, Construction, Repair	Medical, heath care
	Education: teaching English	Relief and development
	Orphans, Orphanages	Orphans, orphanages
	Vision Trip	Vision trip, Prayer Walk
	Relief and Development	Music, worship
	Music, worship	Education: teaching English
	Education: other	Education: other
	Art, Drama	Sports
	Sports	Art, Drama
Least focus	Environment or Justice issues	Environment or justice issues

Table 5.8. Comparison with US Korean Church and Megachurch[22]

Compared with the data from previous studies,[23] the top activity focus of US megachurches is "Building/construction/repair," and for Korean
American churches it is "Evangelism, church planting," which is also a
top-two activity focus for both Chinese churches and megachurches in the
United States. "VBS and children's ministry" is also a top activity focus for
all these churches. Previously we discuss the prioritized ministry concern
in Chinese churches, Korean churches and megachurches in the USA, and
the previous research shows both Korean churches and megachurches have

---

22. Data reported by Hong, "Interracial and Interethnic Attitudes"; and Priest,
Wilson, and Johnson, "New Patterns."

23. Priest, Wilson, and Johnson, "New Patterns," 99; Hong, "Interracial and
Interethnic Attitudes," 89.

"mission to the unreached" and "church planting" as top priorities. Their STM activities seem to agree with their ministry priority, but their destinations are not actually the most unreached areas, as we mentioned in the last section. For Chinese churches these two are the second and third priority next to "missions to Chinese." Although all these churches' STM destinations do not reflect their top priority "missions to the unreached," their activity focus still shows a great emphasis on evangelism and church plating. These studies imply both Chinese and Korean churches focus more on "spiritual" or traditional ministries and direct evangelism, compared with USA megachurches, and Chinese churches focus less on social service and charity.

If we break down the data and see where those Chinese churches that focus on "discipleship training/Bible teaching" sent their STM teams in 2012, we find the majority of them (46 out of 68 churches) sent at least one STM team to China. It shows that Chinese churches in the USA with the advantage of language can have more in-depth ministry like Bible study, teaching and training when they do STM in China. Miriam Adeney's comment on the STM by Chinese Christians in North America is quite accurate: they practice "STM as Bible teaching and discipleship training in China" – overseas Chinese Christians teach or preach the Bible to the Chinese in mainland China.[24] Due to the political situation in China, Chinese Christians in the mainland have limited resources to receive theological training. In other Chinese societies, such as Singapore, Hong Kong and Taiwan, the government allows seminaries, Bible colleges and Christian organizations, while the PRC government only permits the presence of a few state seminaries. Thus, the need for theological training and education is great in mainland China. In fact, all the Chinese church leaders whom I interviewed told me that their church had sent STM teams to China, and their major tasks were teaching and training. They also pointed out it is not legal to do public evangelism in China, so their STM usually focuses more on small-size Bible teaching and theological training. One of the church leaders I interviewed even mentioned their church founded

---

24. Miriam Adeney, "Being There: Short-Term Missions and Human Need," paper presented at Evangelical Missiological Society Regional Meeting, 30 July – 1 August 2009, hosted by Carl F. H. Henry Center, Trinity Evangelical Divinity School, 2009.

an underground Bible school for a local house church and sponsored that school for three years.

It is noteworthy that those churches that report their activity focus of STM is "discipleship training/teaching Bible" also sent STM teams to non-Chinese countries in 2012 (see figure 5.7). This implies Chinese churches in the USA also sent their STM teams to teach and train the Christian Chinese diaspora in different parts of the world such as Europe and Latin America.

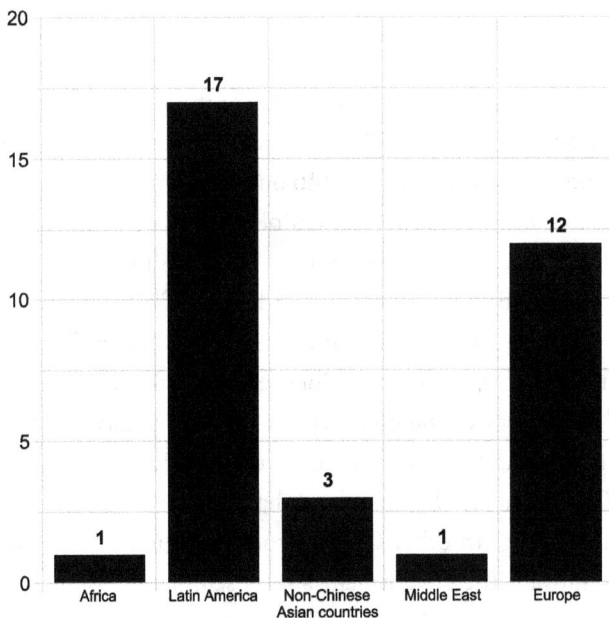

Figure 5.7. STM in 2012 with Activity Focus "Discipleship Training/Teaching Bible"

Besides "discipleship training/teaching Bible," the second most focused activity "evangelism/church planting" also presents a "Chinese first" theme. The data reports that out of the fifty churches that chose "evangelism/church plating" as their activity focus, twenty-six of them have sent at least one STM to the countries or areas with the majority ethnic Chinese in 2012. But the ratio of sending to mainland China is lower (19 out of 50 churches), compared with the churches that answer "discipleship training/teaching Bible." If we look at the activity focus "children's ministry/VBS," the result is similar: twenty-five out of the thirty-nine Chinese churches have sent at least one team to China, Hong Kong or Taiwan, and fifteen of them sent at least one team to mainland China (table 5.8). Some of my informants told me they have co-organized VBS or English camps for children with the local churches in China or Taiwan for years. My home church in the USA also has done this kind of STM for four years.

	Discipleship training/ teaching Bible	Evangelism/ church planting	Children's ministry/ VBS
No. of churches sent STM teams to Chinese countries/ areas in 2012	48 (46 in mainland China)	26 (19 in mainland China)	25 (15 in mainland China)
No. of churches' STM activity focus as listed	68	50	39

Table 5.9. Summary of the Relation between STM Activity Focus and Destinations

How are these tasks accomplished by Chinese STM teams? The C&MA pastor gave us one example on how his church planted churches among Chinese diaspora in other countries through their short-term missions:

> Our principle is that we don't scatter our resources all around, which means we will not change STM destinations every year. We continue to work on one church on the mission field for years, especially if it's the assignment from our denomination or Chinese Churches Association of C & MA in USA. Because our final goal is church planting! Let me take São Paulo, Brazil, as an example. We are only involved in one church there, which is one of the mission fields of Chinese Churches Association of C & MA in USA. We and other Chinese churches are like running a relay race, one baton by one baton. So we roughly spent three or four years in São Paulo, Brazil. We really had the church built up and developed, so they can be independent and self-supporting. To this

point we will have our hands off because our tasks in that stage have been accomplished.

Their way of doing short-term mission is a typical model of diaspora collaboration in missions, and what the diaspora missiologists call "missions through diaspora." It is also remarkable that their denomination plays an important role in assigning their tasks on the mission fields, so the tasks they carry out can meet the needs of the mission fields. Now we have the idea that the STMs carried out by Chinese churches in the USA have different destinations and different tasks compared with USA megachurches and Korean American churches. The next section will focus who are going to these destinations and carrying out these tasks.

Who Is Going?

Previous research on short-term missions discovers that mission pastors play an important role in organizing these mission trips.[25] Yet my research data from chapter 4 shows that less than 1 percent of US Chinese churches have missions pastors, while more than half (51.6%, see previous section) of US Chinese churches send out one or more short-term mission teams every year. It means in US Chinese churches there are other church leaders involved and participating in STM. Since transnational network plays a central role in Chinese short-term missions (see chapter 4), it makes sense that they do not hire mission pastors to take care of mission activities. First of all, US Chinese churches can find transnational connections and mission opportunities through church leaders and members without mission pastors. Second, language skills or cross-cultural experiences, which usually are required for mission pastors in American churches, are not necessary for Chinese short-term missions. As the data shows in chapter 4, most of the pastors (86%) who responded to my survey have gone for overseas short-term mission trips themselves.

Previous research on short-term missions points out the significant involvement of teenagers in the USA in this movement.[26] The research on

---

25. Priest, Wilson, and Johnson, "New Patterns," 101.

26. See for example Tinitapoli and Vaisey, "The Transformative Role," and Jefferey G. MacDonald, "Rise of Sunshine Samaritans: On a Mission of Holiday?" *The Christian Science Monitor*, 25 May 2006.

USA megachurches also shows that 94 percent of their high school youth program have organized overseas short-term mission trips, and 78 percent of them sent more than one youth STM team per year.[27] As a Chinese short-term mission participant, my general perception of the short-term missions by Chinese churches in the USA seems to be a different case. The survey data supports this view. When asking, "How often, if ever, does your congregation's high school youth program organize short-term mission trips abroad," half of the responding Chinese churches in the USA answer "never," and only about 28.7 percent of them send one or more than one youth STM team per year (see figure 5.8). Compared with the frequency of sending general STM teams (see figure 5.1), this is a much lower frequency. This data also shows a very different picture of the STM of the US Chinese church and that of USA megachurches.

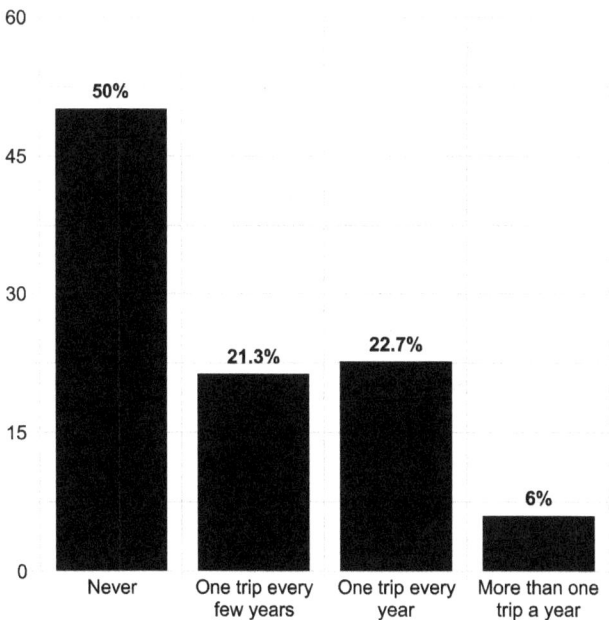

Figure 5.8. The Frequency of Church's High School Youth Program Organizing STM Trips Abroad (N=300)

27. Priest, Wilson, and Johnson, "New Patterns," 98.

So then, who are going for short-term missions in Chinese churches in the USA? A survey on short-term mission for 2012 shows that for those churches that sent STM teams in 2012, 59.1 percent of those churches report that the majority of their STM teams are adults (above 22), while 14 percent of them say the majority of their STM teams are high school youth (see figure 5.9).

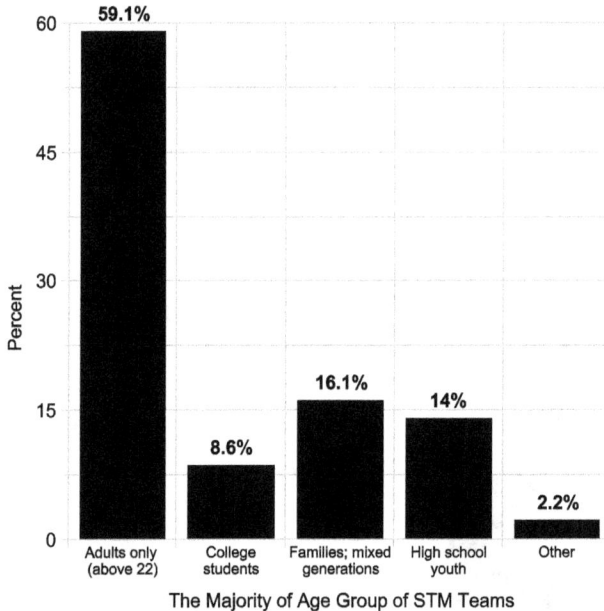

Figure 5.9. *The Majority of Age Group of STM Teams (N=186)*

This result also presents the different tasks and purposes of Chinese diaspora's short-term missions and USA megachurches' short-term mission, because different age groups can have different contributions to the mission field. From previous research and my survey data, we see the different activity focus of Chinese churches compared with the USA megachurches and Korean American churches. How do these different tasks impact the decision of sending people for these churches? When I asked Chinese church leaders about the requirements of being short-term mission team members, all of them answered in the way which relates to the tasks that their STM teams are supposed to accomplish. For example, the C&MA pastor made it very clear and straightforward: they are supposed to be able to carry out all the assignments from their denomination in the mission field, such as evangelism, leading Bible study, leading worship, leading small groups and even preaching. He adds, "at least, every STM team member should have received the training of personal evangelism, home visitation, and of course they can take care of errands, do lots of things." Apparently people who have these kinds of skills are more likely adults, and not only adults, but mature Christians. In this case, C&MA had done the investigation and knew the needs of the field, so they simply assigned this church to help to plant a church among Chinese diaspora in other countries in South America or Europe. In fact, not only this C&MA church, but most of my informants expressed that short-term mission goers need to meet some standard of spiritual life and have some talents or gifts according to the needs of mission field. The elder from the East Coast also explained to me that where their STMs are going decides what their tasks are, and what their tasks are decides who will go: "for example going to China, because we cannot do evangelism and can only do training courses, they need to have the experiences and gifts of teaching, like pastors, elders and adult Sunday school teachers." Later he told me that there are seven elders in their church, and all of them have been on short-term missions.

In previous sections, we showed that most Chinese churches in the USA are sending STM teams to China, and in China most of tasks are Bible teaching and discipleship training; thus it makes sense that most of these short-term mission goers are actually church leaders. My own home church is also a good example: my church does not have a mission pastor, yet all four of our pastors and two of our elders have gone on short-term mission trips; additionally, two of the pastors and one elder have gone to China every year since 2008. This data may also explain the finding that 86 percent of the respondents who are pastors have gone on short-term mission trips (see chapter 4), and most of them have gone on STM trips in China (110 out of the 179 pastors who have done STM). Some previous studies in North American STM point out that the short-term mission participants do not necessarily know the Bible better than the receiving local believers;[28]

---

28. Priest, "Short-Term Mission," 90.

apparently it is quite a different situation for the STMs carried out by Chinese churches in the USA.

But this does not mean Chinese churches in the USA only send very talented and gifted Christians for their short-term mission. The pastor of Bread of Life Christian Church provided a very different answer. He said, "Basically, we simply want someone who believes in Jesus! Because they can learn after they arrive there and someone can teach them so they can be trained on their own." This pastor later explained that their short-term missions focus more on orphanages and summer camps. Some other informants also mentioned they did send youth for short-term mission for English camp, children's ministry or charity/service project. The interview data suggests that the tasks and purposes of the short-term missions determine who will go.

Positive/Negative Impact and Effectiveness

How do Chinese churches in the USA view short-term missions in general? In the questionnaire survey, I gave open-ended questions on the positive and negative impact of short-term missions in their church. Among the 192 churches that answered this questions, 103 of them gave an answer related to "more passionate/care/aware of missions and evangelism," and 85 of them mentioned something related to "spiritual growth, loving/knowing/experiencing God." The previous studies on North American short-term missions[29] discuss extensively on how STM benefits the participants (usually youth in their studies) on their spiritual growth, and some criticize this kind of self-centered mission trip. For Chinese churches in the USA, although spiritual growth is also mentioned frequently, they seem to be more interested in how short-term missions can be mission training or learning opportunities for their congregation, and to mobilize their church members to be involved in the Great Commission.

---

29. See for example, Miriam Adeney, "Shalom Tourist: Loving Your Neighbor While Using Her," in *Missiology* 34, no. 4 (2006): 463–476; Fran Blomberg, "From 'Whatever' to Wherever: Enhancing Faith Formation in Young Adults through Short-Term Missions," in *Effective Engagement in Short-Term Missions: Doing It Right!*, ed. Robert Priest (Pasadena, CA: William Carey Library, 2008); Kurt Ver Beek, "International Service-Learning: A Call to Caution, in *Commitment and Connection: Service-Learning and Christian Higher Education*, eds. Gail Gunst Heffner and Claudia DeVries Beversluis (New York, NY: University Press of America, 2002); Trinitapoli and Vaisey, "The Transformative Role."

Positive Impact of STM in the Church	No. of Churches
More aware of/care for God's missions	103
Spiritual life growth	85
More involved and committed in home church	24
Produce long-term missionaries	18
Improve personal gifts and get more practice and training	17
Realize that they are blessed by abundant material life	12
More willing to give or to support ministry financially	9

Table 5.10. Positive Impact of STM according to the Church Leaders

Another interesting thing is that quite a few churches also mentioned short-term mission is helpful for "producing long-term missionaries." In fact, all the Chinese church leaders I interviewed told me that in the church they have served there were several people responding to the call of being career missionaries after doing short-term missions. The reason might be that I interviewed those church leaders whose churches have better-developed mission programs and have organized short-term mission trips for a longer time. Thus their churches are more likely to produce long-term missionaries through short-term missions. However, this research data cannot show if short-term mission actually helps US Chinese churches to produce more missionaries (i.e. whether they have more long-term missionaries because of doing short-term mission), since there is no data of missionary numbers from the past to compare with the present.[30]

---

30. A study on 690 American Protestant Mission Agencies shows that there was not a significant increase of long-term missionaries between 1996 and 2001, while short-term missionaries increased greatly (see Priest et al., "Researching," 432). Another study during the time between 1992 and 2005 also reports there was not much increase of American full-time overseas missionaries, while the number of support staff of short-term mission grew significantly (see Scott Moreau, "Short-Term Missions in the Context of Missions, Inc.," in *Effective Engagement in Short-Term Missions: Doing It Right!*, ed. Robert Priest (Pasadena, CA: William Carey Library, 2008), 4, 12).

Negative Impact of STM in the Church	No. of Churches
No negative impact	84
Cost lots of money	16
Cannot really accomplish much	13
Cause conflicts and tension in church	12
Take too much work and human resources	7
More like tourism/sight-seeing	6
Cause confusion about missions	5
STM-goers not involved in home church	4
Cause spiritual pride of the STM-goers	3

Table 5.11. Negative Impact of STM according to the Church Leaders

From the 154 responding churches, 84 of them said "there is no negative impact on church." A lot of them mentioned the cost of money, time and human resources, and the that STM teams cannot really accomplish much or meet their expectation in a short time. In fact, most of these negative effects mentioned by Chinese churches are not the major critiques of American short-term missions from previous research, with the exception of the cost and the similarity with tourism. Adeney studies the topic of tourism ethics and analyzes it in three kinds of encounters: physical, cultural, and spiritual. She studies how tourism develops and how it changes people, both the locals and the visitors. Although she criticizes tourism for its costs and harms, she believes Christians can travel differently to bring blessings. She asks, "How shall we travel to the glory of God?"[31] In this way, Adeney puts short-term mission in the category of tourism in spite of their difference in function and activities. According to the survey data, the top ten destinations of the STM by Chinese churches in the USA are somewhat similar to the USA tourists' top ten (see table 5.3). From my observation, it is not uncommon that Chinese STM-goers visit their families in China or do sight-seeing in Europe after their tasks are done. As long as their missions are done, and they pay the expenses of personal traveling from their own pocket, usually it will not cause problems.

---

31. Adeney, "Shalom Tourist," 472.

If we look at the negative impact mentioned by the respondents, we will find some of the answers contradict the answers regarding positive impact. Some of them mentioned that STM caused tension and conflicts in church because of fighting for their agenda, and even caused the spiritual pride of the participants, while some other churches said STM improved participants' spiritual life and made them closer to God. Some churches said the STM-goers only like to serve during STM, but are not involved in the ministries of their home church, while some other churches said STM makes them more committed and willing to serve in church. Some churches mentioned that STM brings misunderstanding or a wrong attitude toward missions, such as confusing social service with sharing the gospel, or viewing making converts as making disciples. Yet some other churches suggest that STM is good for educating their congregation to know about missions. With all these diverse comments on short-term missions, it implies that the effectiveness of short-term missions varies from church to church. Some churches' STM programs may be more successful than others. But overall, there are many more positive comments than negative.

These comments and feedback are merely based on the impact on their own churches, not the impact on the mission field. From previous sections we learned that the short-term missions carried out by Chinese churches in the USA are different from general American short-term missions in various ways, such as destinations, tasks, participants and target people. Do these differences make Chinese short-term missions more effective in the mission fields? A Chinese article in the journal published by the Chinese mission agency "Gospel Operation International" discusses the purpose and function of short-term missions in the Chinese context. The author is a Chinese Malaysian, who became a long-term missionary after participating in short-term missions. Based on his observations and experiences, he summaries that (overseas) Chinese churches usually send STM teams for three purposes: (1) to give more opportunities for the lay believers to participate in missions, so the awareness, mobilization and the involvement of missions can be improved; (2) to support and provide resources for the local missionaries or churches; (3) for those churches that have long-term plans to produce more long-term missionaries through STM.[32] One of my informants, the Chinese pastor in Illinois , mentioned that his church has been debating the first view and second view: for the church versus for the mission field. He further elaborated how he evaluated their short-term missions from these two viewpoints:

> The first view is that STM is for church's mission education . . . The second view is that STM is for the local missionaries, and from this view it is quite effective. Almost every time the local missionaries feel it is very helpful when we go to there. So it is very effective. I said earlier that my view is STM is educational. STM should play an important role on this . . . So from this point of view, I feel it has not reached the goal yet . . . To promote the "awareness of mission and knowledge of mission should be enhanced by short-term mission ministry," from this aspect I feel we still have a lot to do. (Chinese pastor in Illinois)

It is interesting that this pastor thinks that their short-term missions are more effective on the receiving side rather than the sending side. Many recent studies on American short-term missions have mentioned critiques that the STM trips were designed for short-termers' spiritual benefits and not for the local people;[33] however, this Chinese pastor in Illinois suggests that their short-term mission is "very helpful" for the local people, but not as helpful for their own congregation. Another one of my informants, the C&MA pastor, thinks short-term missions still benefit the participants the most, but he also believes it is helpful for the receiving local church or people in some degree. He explains how their short-term missions are effective to the local people or churches:

> STM from some points of view, still benefits the goers most . . . When we did STM, most of the time the local missionaries were also involved, and we co-worked with them. They

---

32. Andrew Chai, "Short-Term Missions: Do You Take It Seriously?" (短宣: 你是認真的嗎?) *Gospel Operation International* (華傳), 21 (May–June 2013), http://gointl.org/gointl_portal/publication/magazine/article/1574

33. Adeney, "Shalom Tourist"; Wuthnow, *Boundless Faith.*

knew their needs very well, like helping them to plant the church, or that church was just planted and had some special needs in that stage . . . then we delivered as much as possible according to their needs and design. Although people often say, "what can you do in just one or two weeks?" my viewpoint is more like, since we always cooperate with the local missionaries, and they know well how to use these STM teams – request what kind of talents they need, and then use our talents. So I will say from the ministry's perspective, I believe STM certainly has some contributions to the church planting. I'm not sure about how big is the contribution, but definitely there is some . . . So I look at the question from two aspects: to the STM-goers, certainly they receive most benefits from their spiritual growth. But to the local ministry, I believe it also has some contribution, because we are not doing it according to our own desire, nor our plans, but the plan of the local missionaries. (Chinese C&MA pastor in the Midwest)

It is noteworthy that these church leaders whom I interviewed are selected because they themselves have much experience of short-term missions, and this implies that their churches are also more experienced in STM. All of them shared with me the procedures of the STM programs of their churches: they usually have the process of applications, fundraising or preparation, training and debriefings. The church leaders also think through the goals and purposes of the trips before they go. In other words, their short-term missions are well planned. With strategies, preparation, training programs and follow-up debriefings, their short-term missions can be more effective than some other Chinese churches in the USA, besides the advantage of language and culture which they all share. Although these selective church leaders cannot speak for all Chinese churches in the USA, their ways of doing short-term missions still help us to know how overseas Chinese short-term missions are different or similar to mainstream American short-term missions.

When talking about the North American short-term mission movement, Edwin Zehner comments that "discussion of the perspectives of the local host of these missions is still rare."[34] I had the same impression when searching for articles and books on the topic of Western short-term mission. One possible reason is language barrier. Whether qualitative or quantitative research, it has to be conducted in the local language. My research data shows that most short-term missions done by Chinese churches in the USA are to ethnic Chinese people in mainly Chinese countries. In other words, most of them are not cross-cultural missions. In this case, would it not be easier to know the response and feedback from the local people who received the short-term mission teams, and what kind of response they had?

All my informants generally reported very positive responses from the receiving communities when asked. The local people or churches appreciate their presence and the ministries they provided. Like the two pastors I quoted earlier, they are pretty confident about the local people's positive feedback especially when the people they minister to are ethnic Chinese. Their confidence may come from the knowledge of Chinese culture and the Chinese way of communication. "They asked us when we would come back!" This kind of question/invitation is evidence that their STM teams are welcomed there. In most cases, their churches sent STM teams to support the ministries of local missionaries or local churches, and/or to organize special events like summer camps, evangelistic rallies, social service or theology/Bible training courses. When asked about how the local Chinese people in mainland China respond to their short-term missions, the Chinese pastor from a Lutheran church in California said:

> They generally welcome overseas Chinese to work with them
> . . . In addition, we speak their language, which brings great
> closeness and makes things easier. If it is (Caucasian) Americans
> . . . they may feel it is interesting in the beginning, but very
> soon, because of the barrier of language, they can't continue
> to work with them. Thus they welcome us, and also the local
> missionaries welcome us. The reason is if it's American, the lo-
> cal missionaries need to be their interpreters and tour guides,

---

34. Edwin Zehner, "Short-Term Missions: Toward a More Field-Oriented Model," *Missiology* 34, no. 4 (2006): 510.

and have to arrange everything for them. Sometimes missionaries would think that they prefer them not to come, because
they (American STM teams) will interrupt all their works and
they need to put away their works to entertain them and to
help them. But when we go, we totally arrange everything
on our own because we are more familiar with China, Hong
Kong and Taiwan. We can say, "You don't need to make the
arrangement since we can do it on our own" . . . For example,
some of us are ABC – American-Born Chinese, then we don't
need the missionaries to be interpreters, because our people
can be interpreters. So the local missionaries don't need to
take care of us at all. They can take a break. (Chinese Lutheran
pastor in California)

Unfortunately, the response of the local missionaries in China might
testify to some of the critiques of American short-term missions in recent
research, such as the lack of good relationships with the local people,[35]
and that short-term mission teams add burdens and work for the host
communities in many ways, e.g. accommodation, meals, transportation,
translation, etc.[36] On the other hand, we also need to notice that the local receiving communities generally only report the positive side of their
experiences with the STM teams. For example, according to a few studies on the local experiences in Latin America,[37] the receiving communities
generally have positive views of the short-term mission teams. Most of the
local people (67%) "believe short-term mission brings some benefits to the
national church";[38] they also show much willingness to host the foreign

---

35. Adeney, "When the Elephant Dances."

36. Zehner, "Short-Term Missions"; Miriam Adeney, "The Myth of the Blank Slate: A
Check-List for Short-Term Missions," in *Effective Engagement in Short-Term Missions: Doing
It Right!*, ed. Robert Priest (Pasadena, CA: William Carey Library, 2008).

37. Martín Hartwig Eitzen, "Short-Term Missions: A Latin American Perspective,"
Journal of Latin American Theology: Christian Reflections from the Latino South 2 (2007);
Joaquin Alegre Villon, "Short-Term Missions: Experiences and Perspectives from Callao,
Peru," *Journal of Latin American Theology: Christian Reflections from the Latino South* 2
(2007); Rodrigo Maslucán, "Short-Term Missions: Analysis and Proposals," *Journal of Latin
American Theology: Christian Reflections from the Latino South* 2: (2007).

38. Eitzen, "Latin American Perspective," 38.

team members;[39] the local church considers the visit of the mission team is "a great blessing";[40] they believe their goal had been "100% reached" and "made a big impact on the community";[41] and both the receiving and sending groups are benefited.[42] But the context of mainland China is very different from Latin America regarding the politics and religious restrictions of the PRC. A Western face indeed draws attention and may cause some inconvenience or trouble to the local churches in mainland China. Overall, this Chinese Lutheran pastor's experiences in China still can support the relevance and effectiveness of "mission through diaspora."

In sum, all the research data – both survey and interviews – suggests that Chinese Christians in the USA take advantage of language and culture when carrying out short-term missions to their own kinsmen in various parts of the world. According to their self-evaluation, the short-term missions done by Chinese churches in the USA can be very effective when done with strategy – targeting the right field with tasks that meet the needs of the locals, pre-trip trainings and follow-up debriefing.

Evaluation of Short-Term Missions by Chinese Diaspora

Evangelistic Efforts

When thinking about mission, what first comes to mind may be activities like evangelism, church planting, Bible studies, etc. Short-term mission as a kind of mission may be also expected to have these kind of spiritual activities. Thus, first of all, we will examine the evangelistic effect of short-term mission.

The previous studies on USA megachurches report the top primary activity is "building, construction and repair."[43] But if looking carefully where these American STM teams serve, research shows that they mostly go to the "World C" – countries or areas that are most "evangelized"

---

39. Ibid., 44.
40. Villon, "Experiences and Perspectives," 131.
41. Ibid., 132.
42. Maslucán, "Analysis and Proposals," 143.
43. Priest, Wilson, and Johnson, "New Patterns," 99.

and churches are already present.[44] This previous research points out that the major task of American short-term missions is not "reaching the least reached." As for the short-term missions done by Chinese churches, we discover from research data that Chinese churches in the USA are sending most of their STM teams to World B (e.g. China), and then World C (e.g. Germany); World A (e.g. Middle East) still receives the least STM teams.

However, the top prioritized concern of ministry of Chinese is not "missions to the unreached," but "missions to Chinese." When we look at their STM destinations, we find these places are either with majority Chinese or large Chinese immigration population. In other words, most Chinese churches in the USA are not sending STMs based on whether these areas are World B or World C, but the needs of the local Chinese. And since these areas already have the presence of churches, their STM teams usually work with the local churches or missionaries. Without language and culture barriers, they can take on many tasks and witness to the non-believers directly. The Baptist pastor in Texas shared his experiences of personal evangelism in China with me:

> If you're talking about receiving the Lord, so far till now it's pretty much the same way in China: if you have the chance to talk about the Four Spiritual Laws to the locals, 70% of them would believe the Lord. In 1997 and 1998 when I just started to go to China, at that time you shared with one and then one would believe – it's almost 100% of them would believe Jesus. Now the economics in China is getting better so people don't feel so depressed in their hearts, they have lots of money to buy the stuff they desire, and they're well fed, everything is fine, so the desire of spiritual things and God is not that strong. So now about 7 of 10 will believe. And it's almost like if you have the chance to talk to him, he will believe. It's roughly 70%. And in the first year I went we also perhaps had 20-ish people believing in Jesus in that English class. (Chinese Baptist pastor in Texas)

---

44. Priest, "Short-Term Mission," 90; Adeney, "Blank Slate," 124.

It is impressive that they can convert so many people in one STM trip. But this kind testimony is not unusual in a typical kind of STM by Chinese churches in the USA when reaching national Chinese or overseas Chinese. The short-term mission teams from my home church, of which I have been a part, have all experienced this kind of "ready harvest" when doing evangelism. In light of this, the short-term missions done by Chinese churches in the USA are effective in their evangelistic effort, although often they are not reaching the least reached, but their kinsmen.

Spiritual Impact

It is not uncommon to hear short-term mission participants share in debriefings how much they were encouraged or how their faith has been refreshed from their experience. In the article, "From 'Whatever' to Wherever: Enhancing Faith Formation in Young Adults through Short-Term Missions," Fran Blomberg uses the theories of Erikson, Fowler, and Parks to examine the spiritual development of young adults and analyze how short-term mission trips can build them up.[45] On the study of experiences of short-term college mission teams, David Johnstone also advocates the positive influence which short-term cross-cultural service brings to young people, emphasizing the importance of debriefings.[46] In the case of US Chinese churches, they actually do not send as many youth on overseas mission trips, but adults. So is it still true that short-term mission is an effective way to help Chinese Christians to grow in their faith and spiritual life?

Many studies on American short-term missions talk about the spiritual influence of short-term missions, especially on young people.[47] But other research also finds that there is a great difference between qualitative and quantitative results: qualitative research usually reports great spiritual change after STM while quantitative research does not. The reason may be either the questionnaires are not able to measure the change of

---

45. Blomberg, "From 'Whatever' to Wherever," 593–596.

46. David M. Johnstone, "Closing the Loop: Debriefing and the Short-Term College Missions Team," *Missiology* 34, no. 4 (2006).

47. Blomberg, "From 'Whatever' to Wherever"; Johnstone, "Closing the Loop"; Trinitapoli and Vaisey, "The Transformative Role."

life, or the self-perception of life change is much greater than the reality.[48] Considering how long this spiritual influence lasts, some research results show that short-term mission trips "tend to produce temporary changes only."[49] Considering how American STM impacts personal response to the calling of long-term missionaries, previous research reports that short-term mission did not significantly increase long-term missionaries.[50] According to Robert Priest's research data, the number of Christian short-term mission goers has been rapidly increasing from 1996 to 2001, while the number of long-term missionaries has not changed much.[51]

According to my research data, both the questionnaire survey and interviews report the spiritual growth of both adults and youth as a positive impact of STM. Many of my informants told me how their church members are inspired and encouraged by the STM trips and would like to go back. It is noteworthy that the majority of the respondents and all the informants are church leaders, which means that they know their congregation well. Thus their comments are not merely a self-perception but a long-term observation in their church. However, it is hard to judge whether the short-term missions by Chinese churches in the USA bring greater spiritual impact on the participants, because the more positive results may come from different research methodology. Additionally, my research method cannot measure how long the spiritual impact lasted.

Cultural Encounter

Since overseas short-term missions takes place somewhere outside the USA, some cross-cultural experiences are expected. Miriam Adeney raises some key critiques of American short-term mission such as: the lack of respect and sensitivity to the local culture, tending to impose American values upon the receiving communities, and causing hurt.[52] On the other hand, Edwin Zehner considers American short-term mission as "a new paradigm of cross-cultural relation" in his article.[53] Is short-term mission carried out

---

48. Ver Beek, "Lessons from the Sapling," 489.
49. Priest et al., "Researching," 444.
50. Priest et al., "Researching"; Moreau, "Context of Missions."
51. Priest et al., "Researching."
52. Adeney, "When the Elephant Dances."
53. Zehner, "Rhetoric."

by Chinese churches in the USA effective in the sense of increasing real cultural experiences?

First of all, the research data shows that most of the short-term missions carried out by Chinese churches in the USA actually takes place in the areas with the ethnic Chinese majority – mainland China, Hong Kong, Macau, Taiwan and Singapore. Some of the STM participants actually come from China or Taiwan. In this case, the STM participants will not have cross-cultural experience since it is just like traveling to their home, not a foreign country. For some other people, they may still experience some cultural differences – like those American-born (second generation) Chinese going to China, or mainland Chinese going to Taiwan or Singapore – but these cultures are still considered relatively similar, and these cultural differences mainly come from different political regimes.[54]

Furthermore, only about 9 percent of Chinese churches reported that their overseas STM primarily ministered to non-Chinese, and these churches include those who sent STM teams to Europe, Latin America and Africa (see chapter 4). For those STM teams traveling to Europe, Latin America or Africa to minister to Chinese diaspora, although they were in a country of different culture, their cultural experiences might be very minimal because during the trip very likely they only spent time with the local Chinese. From the interviews, I found out that their short-term mission teams only had basic observation and understanding on the culture of their STM destinations. Even for those STM teams going to other countries to minister to non-Chinese – for example, some of my informants told me their church sent youth to Mexico to build houses for the local people – they still did not report many cultural experiences.

In sum, the research data shows that most short-term mission carried out by Chinese churches in the USA lacks real cross-cultural experience. The positive side is that they may not make as many cultural mistakes as American short-term mission teams, since they mainly deal with Chinese people. The negative side is that their short-term mission teams may not have the chance to experience, learn and appreciate a different kind of

---

54. Peng, *Culture and Conflict*, 33–34; Ringo Ma, "Communication Experiences and Adaptation of Mainland Chinese in Hong Kong and Hong Kong Chinese in Mainland China," *Journal of Intercultural Communication Research* 38, no. 2 (2009): 119.

culture. However, cross-cultural experience is not the only way to carry out the Great Commission; Jesus commissioned the church to be his witnesses in Jerusalem and Judea, as well as to the ends of the earth (Acts 1:8). As diaspora missiology has emphasized, less or no cultural and linguistic barrier is a unique advantage of this kind of mission approach. Diaspora Chinese can be considerably more effective than non-Chinese in doing short-term missions among ethnic Chinese. Both cross-cultural mission and near-cultural mission have a role to play in God's mission, and different kinds of people groups (i.e. World A and World B) require different approaches to reach and disciple all nations. While cross-cultural mission is necessary for pioneer missions among World A unreached people groups, near-cultural mission such as that undertaken by the diaspora Chinese church can be strategic for reaching the large World B ethnic Chinese population.

Social Engagement

From previous research on North American short-term missions, we see most short-term mission teams are sent to less wealthy countries, and social service is one of the major activities, which is evidence that short-term mission movement in the West is responding to the call of social responsibility in many ways. Short-term mission is effective in connecting Western Christians with social others,[55] but it does not change the participants' behaviors of materialism to a significant degree.[56]

The survey data (see previous section) shows that many US Chinese churches send short-term mission teams to the UK, Germany, Taiwan, Hong Kong and China, and there is not always a significant economic difference between the US and these destinations of the STM of US Chinese churches. As for the case of mainland China, as I mentioned earlier, it depends on the city to which they go. In addition, for these Chinese Christians who are new immigrants or perhaps not even naturalized yet, they do not necessarily have the kind of Western mindset of "feeling guilty for some part of the world."[57] This also shows on the result of the sur-

---

55. Priest, "Short-Term Mission."

56. Priest et al., "Researching," 440.

57. Richard Slimbach, "The Mindful Missioner," in *Effective Engagement in Short-Term Missions: Doing It Right!*, ed. Robert Priest (Pasadena, CA: William Carey Library, 2008), 163.

vey: a low percentage of Chinese churches' STM activity focus is "building, construction, repair," "orphanage" or "relief and development," which agrees with the fact that only 5.9 percent and 2.4 percent of US Chinese churches report "poverty" and "social justice" as their ministry top priority. This suggests that social engagement is not the main concern of their short-term missions.

On the other hand, most of my informants still recognize the fact that they and their church members do live a more materially abundant life living in the United States. The census data also shows that Chinese in the USA have higher income and education than the average (see chapter 4). The survey data does report some positive impact of STM related to material life such as "feeling blessed and grateful for what they have," or "more willing to give and support ministry financially." Several Chinese churches also responded in the survey that their church was supporting some overseas churches financially. But overall, the research data implies that compared with other American churches, the involvement and engagement of US Chinese churches on social issues is still limited and on the surface level. For US Chinese churches, the transnational ties (i.e. social connections) come before social concerns. However, both the Old and New Testaments repeatedly address social issues and caring for the poor, orphans and widows (Deut 10:18; Isa 1:17; Jas 1:27). Therefore, US Chinese churches have room for growth in how they reflect these biblical priorities in their mission practice.

Relationships with the Receiving Communities

There have been critiques about "the lack of good relationships with the local people" pointed out in previous research on American short-term mission,[58] while some articles written by the receiving side report a generally positive view on American short-term missions and point out that what the local people value most is the relationship with the short-term mission team rather than the material benefits.[59] How do the receiving communities view short-term mission by Chinese churches in the USA?

---

58. Adeney, "When the Elephant Dances."

59. Eitzen, "Latin American Perspective"; Villon, "Experiences and Perspectives"; Maslucán, "Analysis and Proposals."

Is short-term mission by Chinese churches effective in the way it builds up relationships and partnership with the receiving church or community?

My research data shows that most of the short-term mission teams sent by US Chinese churches are actually working among ethnic Chinese people. Thus, the STM team members can communicate with the local people or missionaries without a language barrier and they may not add too much work and burden on the receiving communities. As some of my informants pointed out, they need to be very sensitive, low key and careful when working in mainland China due to the political situation. In this kind of case, the STM teams and the local church need to trust each other when doing ministry together. If the US Chinese church works with house churches (underground churches), they would only send a small team of two or three people to China. This kind of small team is flexible, not dominating, and will not burden the receiving side too much. Also, usually the activities of the STM are designed for meeting the needs of the locals. As mentioned earlier, all my informants told me that the local people have a positive response to their short-term mission and appreciate their works; one also mentioned that some of their STM team members maintain personal contact with the local people to whom they ministered or with whom they worked. Moreover, the survey data shows that almost 60 percent of Chinese churches always or often send STM teams repeatedly to the same destinations. This also implies there is a good relationship between the sending and receiving side. But as for partnership, the survey data shows it is still not very common among US Chinese churches to have partnership with churches in other countries.

As the survey data and interview data report, *guanxi* (personal relationship and connection) and transnational networks are the key of short-term missions in a Chinese context. In fact, all the church leaders mentioned that their STM to some place is started with some kind *"guanxi"* with the local church or community. In the Chinese context, relationship – *guanxi* – is crucial. If the sending church and the receiving community do not have *guanxi*, the ministry will not happen. In light of this, short-term missions done by US Chinese churches present different characteristics from American churches. From a biblical point of view, mission is not merely about programs or projects. It is more about the people who get involved in it, and more about souls and lives. Building up good relationships is the essence of mission itself.

Summary

Through this evaluation on the short-term missions by Chinese churches in the USA, we find, first, their short-term mission is strong and effective in evangelism, not to least-reached people, but to the non-believing Chinese. Second, the research results also suggest that church leaders are generally positive about the spiritual impact that the short-term missions can bring to their church members. The church leaders report there have been church members becoming long-term missionaries after going for a short-term mission trip. Third, as for cultural experiences, most of their short-term mission teams do not have the chance to have a full experience of another culture because often they either do short-term missions in Chinese societies, or minister to ethnic Chinese people. On the other hand, it also avoids some cross-cultural conflicts and mistakes. Fourth, the Chinese churches in the USA usually do not send their short-term mission teams for social engagement. They recognize their privilege of living in the USA, and they do give financial support to the churches of other countries, but the social engagement is still minimal. Fifth, Chinese churches in the USA generally have a good relationship with the receiving community, and their short-term mission teams usually are welcomed to go back repeatedly.

The short-term missions done by US Chinese churches have different strengths and weaknesses compared with other North American short-term missions. Unlike American churches, which tend to do short-term missions in places of shorter distance (e.g. Latin America), Chinese churches choose to minister to the people of less difference (i.e. their own kinsmen). The Chinese short-term mission shows significant transnational ties and plays an important role of "mission through diaspora" and diaspora collaboration in mission work, while American short-term mission plays an important role in connecting Christians from different social conditions and building up relationships. No matter if it is Chinese or American, short-term mission is not a short-cut mission. The trip itself can be short, but efforts of following-up and partnership effort should be long-term. There is no short cut for discipleship training, cross-cultural understanding, social reconciliation, trustworthy relationship and spiritual transformation.

CHAPTER 6

Implications and Conclusion

The two-fold purpose of this study is as follows: (1) to help Chinese Christians and church leaders in the USA better understand the state of US Chinese mission practice, including strengths and weaknesses, and (2) to contribute to missiological research in diaspora missiology and short-term missions, showing how the US Chinese church helps illumine and expand these fields. This chapter draws together the conclusions of this research, showing how the implications of this study help illuminate the diaspora mission practice of the US Chinese church for both US Chinese Christians and academic researchers of diaspora and short-term mission.

Three Mission Stages of Chinese Churches in the USA

The strategy of Chinese mission proposed by Zephaniah Yu, the director of Gospel Operation International may provide the best description of the progressional way of doing missions of the US Chinese churches: "Local Local," "Local Global,"[1] "Global Local" and "Global Global" (see chapter 1). They want to start with convenient and near missions to motivate and educate their congregation for missions, and hope to move forward to the cross-cultural missions. According to the findings of this dissertation, we find there are three stages in the way US Chinese churches doing missions:[2]

---

1. This research did not collect the data related to "Local Global" missions.
2. The term "stage" is used here to refer to spiritual and missional development in line with the progressional diaspora missiology.

1) Local Local (mission through diaspora)

US Chinese churches at this stage focus on outreach to ethnic Chinese people such as new immigrants, international students and workers in their community, but they have not organized overseas short-term mission trips on their own. Previous studies show that this kind of "Local Local" mission has brought about the growth of Chinese churches in the USA in the last two decades. According to research data, about 28 percent of US Chinese churches that report they have not sent short-term mission teams can be classified to this stage. The research data shows that USA churches that have not done STMs are less likely to support overseas long-term missionaries, or support less long-term missionaries ($r= 0.401, p < 0.01$); churches at this stage also are more like to be smaller in size ($r=0.551, p <0.01$).

2) Global Local (mission through diaspora)

US Chinese churches at this stage organize short-term mission trips to ethnic Chinese in mainland China, Hong Kong, Taiwan or other non-Chinese countries. At the same time they still reach out to Chinese people in their community. The data shows that for the churches that had organized short-term mission trips in 2012,[3] about 69 percent of them primarily ministered to ethnic Chinese. Therefore the majority of US Chinese churches that send short-term missions are at the stage of "Global Local." The research data also shows that churches that sent short-term missions to minister to Chinese are also more likely to see "missions to Chinese" as high priority of their ministry ($r=-0.277, p <0.01$).

3) Global Global (mission by/beyond diaspora)

US Chinese churches at this stage organize short-term mission trips not only to their kinsmen, but also people of other ethnicities in other countries. The data shows that for the churches that had organized short-term mission trips in 2012, about 22 percent of them ministered to both ethnic Chinese and non-Chinese, and 9 percent of them primarily ministered to non-Chinese. Compared with those churches that practice short-term missions to ethnic Chinese, these churches that reach out to non-Chinese

---

3. About 60% of the US Chinese churches report that they had sent out short-term mission teams in 2012.

are more likely to support more overseas long-term missionaries ($r=0.232$, $p <0.01$), and also their long-term missionaries are less likely to minister to Chinese ($r=-0.291$, $p <0.01$). They are more likely to prioritize ministries of "evangelizing the Muslim world," "missions to unreached" and "poverty," instead of "missions to Chinese." Furthermore, these churches are more likely to have a larger size ($r=0.172$, <0.05), spend more money generally ($r=0.288$, $p <0.01$) and on overseas ministries ($r=0.270$, $p <0.01$), and have more church members who have gone on STM trips in 2012 ($r=168$, $p <0.05$).

The research data shows that the majority of US Chinese churches are practicing "mission through diaspora," and the data implies that most churches are at the second stage, practicing "Global Local" mission. The data also implies that US Chinese churches that are practicing "Global Global" mission are more likely larger in size and better-developed, and they are less likely to see "missions to Chinese" as a top priority. This finding agrees with the progressional way of understanding and practicing mission of Chinese churches, as Wan, Yu and most of my informants proposed.

Missiological Implications & Recommendations for Chinese Churches

This research is an investigation of the mission activities of Chinese churches in the USA, attempting to test the general idea of the way US Chinese churches engage in missions (i.e. "Chinese first" or "reach out to our kinsmen") and to test the diaspora missiology theory of "mission to/through/ beyond diaspora." The research data proves that this general perception of the Chinese way of doing mission is accurate, and that diaspora mission is relevant and practical in the Chinese context. Through the comparison with the previous studies on US megachurches and US Korean churches, we can clearly see that with the advantage of language and culture, the focus and priority of the mission activities of US Chinese churches are on the innumerable ethnic Chinese around the world.

How are we to understand this "Chinese first" focus and priority? Before I started this research project, my reasoning for the mission approach of Chinese churches was simply "ethnocentrism." But after careful research, I discovered that the cause behind this kind of mission practice is more complicated than ethnocentrism. The diaspora theories in many ways help us to understand how a diaspora group is formed and how they relate themselves with their homeland. In the case of Chinese diaspora, we find that the manner in which they do their missions from various aspects is shaped by the special political situation in mainland China and its relationship with the Chinese diaspora. The regime change in China in 1949 has increased the population of the Chinese diaspora in Hong Kong, Taiwan, Southeast Asia and North America, and overseas Chinese Christians in these areas have a burden for their homeland due to the lack of religious freedom in the PRC. Due to the shortage of theological education and Bible institutions in mainland China, overseas Chinese churches provide human and financial resources for the enormous number of house churches, and also practice the "STM as Bible teaching in China." At the same time, the overseas Chinese churches, especially in North America, continue to reach out to the newly arrived Chinese students and workers from the PRC in their communities and even in other host countries. This phenomenon validates the theory that diaspora "maintain regular or occasional contacts with what they regard as their homelands and with individuals and groups of the same background residing in other host countries."[4] We can see this kind of transnationalism even more in Chinese short-term missions, and this makes Chinese short-term missions different from American short-term missions.

It is certainly understandable that the largest diaspora group are inclined to reach out and minister to their own people group, which is one-fifth of the world population. In the case of ethnic Chinese, diaspora missiology is relevant and practical. The research data also shows that diaspora Chinese can minister to their own people more efficiently and directly than people of another ethnicity. However, diaspora missiology does not stop with the stage of reaching out to their own kinsmen, but moves forward to other ethnic groups – mission beyond/by diaspora. Today, traditional cross-cultural mission is not viewed as the only type of mission, but it is still needed. The reason is simple: The Lord says "go and make disciples of all nations . .

---

4. Sheffer, "Diaspora Politics," 9–10.

." (Matt 28:19). Yet if all ethnic groups only reach out to their own ethnic groups, who will reach out to the least reached or unreached people in the world? In fact, the research data has shown that those US Chinese churches that see "missions to the unreached" as a higher priority are more likely to spend a higher percentage of money on overseas missions, organize mission conferences more often, and support more long-term missionaries. Furthermore, among all ministry priorities, "evangelizing Muslims" rather than "missions to Chinese," has the most significant correlation with mission activities, which means US Chinese churches that see "evangelizing Muslims" as high priority are more likely to send STM teams and hold mission conferences more frequently, support more long-term missionaries overseas, and spend a higher percentage on overseas ministries. In other words, US Chinese churches that aim for "Global Global" mission are those churches that have well-developed mission programs. This research result also agrees with the spiritual principle that those churches which have a "kingdom mindset" and do not only care about "people of their own kind" are more mature and healthier churches.

Another thing I will add is that when I started to conduct the questionnaire survey and sent an invitation to Chinese churches in the USA, I received many encouraging messages from different Chinese churches. Some of the church leaders are acquaintances of mine, yet most of them I did not know at all. They generally were interested to see the result of this study and showed support for my research. This is just a small sign that US Chinese churches have a desire to grow and learn in the way of doing God's mission.

In light of this study, the following are recommendations for mission practice for Chinese churches in the USA. (1) Start from local missions – first "Local Local" and then move forward to "Local Global";[5] (2) When the church has enough resources, they can utilize the transnational networks from their own church to send short-term mission teams of qualified and trained members to ethnic Chinese (Global Local), while supporting

---

5. This research did not directly measure the involvement of Local Global mission of US Chinese churches. According to the data of languages of their services and interviews with church leaders, the majority of attendees speak either Chinese or English, which implies that the effort of reaching out to local non-Chinese or non-Americans is still minimal.

long-term missionaries who serve among various ethnic groups (Global Global). Speaking in a practical way, it may be unrealistic to expect short-term mission teams to convert local people in the least-reached countries (World A) in a few weeks, where public evangelism is usually against the law. To adjust to a new culture, build up close relationships with local people and have the opportunity to share their faith may take years in some contexts. In light of this, the Chinese church definitely is more efficient in doing short-term missions to their kinsmen in evangelizing, teaching and discipling, and they should continue to do so. (3) STM-goers and long-term missionaries should have debriefing at church when they return. Through doing "Local Global" mission, short-term mission and supporting long-term missionaries in different places, congregations will gain more experience, understanding and passion for God's mission, and with the advantage of being bi-cultural and bilingual, the diaspora Chinese church may produce their own long-term missionaries in the future.

Conclusion

Through this research data we verify the prevalence and effectiveness of modern diaspora mission in the Chinese context. In many ways, missions carried out by the Chinese diaspora today in the globalized world reflects the mission in the first century carried out by Jewish Diaspora in the Roman Empire, and diaspora Jews like the apostle Paul and Barnabas are missionary models of the diaspora Chinese Christians. Further, diaspora cooperation in mission which took place in the book of Acts still happens in the twenty-first century in the Chinese context. Here are four concluding observations from the findings of my research:

1) Both Wan's diaspora missiology and Yu's Chinese mission strategy are applicable to the US Chinese church. Both are a progressional way of doing missions.

2) It is true that the majority of US Chinese churches are doing missions to ethnic Chinese. They also collaborate with other ethnic Chinese in mission works.

3) US Chinese STM is different from American STM in many ways and some of the findings and critiques of American STM cannot apply to US Chinese STM.

4) Diaspora theories can explain the way that US Chinese churches do mission, and this kind of transnationalism in mission already existed economically among diaspora Chinese a long time ago.

Today, according to the recent data of the United Nations, international migrants already reached 214 million,[6] which is about 3 percent of world's population. As Hanciles puts it, "faith spread mainly through kinship and commercial networks, migrant movements (some stimulated by persecution), and other forms of mobility."[7] In fact, mission to/through/by diaspora not only happens to Chinese diaspora. In the book, *A Wind in the House of Islam*, David Garrison mentions how the Korean diaspora in Muslim countries in Central Asia provided "a key cultural bridge" for later Korean missionaries after the Soviet Union fell.[8] This shows that God uses diaspora to spread the gospel and expand his kingdom, not only in the first century, but also today. The Scripture tells us how God has accomplished his mission through/by diaspora throughout the Roman Empire, and he is still working through/by diaspora now in the globalized world. Thus, I believe the beautiful picture of future mission will be that missionaries from different cultures, ethnic groups and geographical regions work together in all different places for the kingdom of God. As in the last days, all those who are purchased *from every tribe and language and people and nation* with the blood of Christ (Rev 5:9) will sing the new song and praise the Lord together.

Suggestions for Further Studies

There are three directions of future studies I would suggest: first, the current overseas mission practices in mainland China as a sending country. There have been a few Chinese house churches (underground churches) who send Christian workers to Central Asia and the Middle East to respond to

---

6. See U.N. Department of Economic and Social Affairs, Global Migration Group 2010.

7. Jehu J. Hanciles. *Beyond Christendom: Globalization, African Migration and the Transformation of the West* (Maryknoll, NY: Orbis Books, 2008), 155.

8. These ethnic Koreans immigrated in Siberia during the 19th century and were relocated to the Soviet Central Asia during WW II (see David Garrison, *A Wind in the House of Islam* [Monument, CO: WIGTake, 2014], 151).

the so-called "Back to Jerusalem Movement," and their Christian identities are covered – some of them do "business as mission" (BAM) – but
the number of these Christian workers is small, and it is hard to identify
them as missionaries.[9] The way Chinese house churches in the PRC do
overseas missions has been a mysterious topic: as Chinese Christians we
have heard people talk about it, such as BAM in Middle East done by the
house churches in Wenzhou, but we never read a study and research about
it even in the Chinese language. Due to the political situation in China,
missions activities are underground, thus it will take a long time to do this
kind of research. It may be a challenging topic to research but will also be
very interesting. The second one is mission practice (including short-term
missions) of Chinese diaspora in other areas, such as Asia, Europe and
Latin America. From my knowledge, there are some Chinese missionaries
from Hong Kong and Southeast Asia in Africa that do outreach among
Chinese workers living there. How they carry out their missions and how
they collaborate with the local African churches or other Chinese churches
may be an interesting study. A third topic for future research is the mission
practice of other diaspora peoples, such as African, Mexican, Lebanese, etc.
Studies like this should be done more widely in different ethnic groups and
different areas.

---

9. Kim-Kong Chan, "Case Study 2: Missiological Implications of Chinese Christians
in Diaspora," in *Diaspora Missiology: Theory, Methodology, and Practice*, ed. Enoch Wan
(Portland, OR: Institute of Diaspora Studies-USA, 2011), 183.

Cover Letter for Survey Package (in English and Chinese)

Dear Pastoral Team,

Greetings in the name of our Lord Jesus Christ!

This letter is to let you know that in two weeks you will be receiving an invitation to participate in a nation-wide survey of Chinese churches in the USA. This survey will focus on the mission activities of Chinese American churches, e.g. supporting missionaries, sending short-term mission teams, hosting mission conferences, etc. While there have been major studies of the mission activities of other churches in America, this will be the first nation-wide study of its kind among Chinese American churches. As a PhD Candidate who speaks both Chinese and English, I will be carrying out this research under the supervision of Dr Robert Priest, Professor of Missions at Trinity Evangelical Divinity School. It is my intention to report on the research in my PhD Dissertation and also write a shorter report for publication. I will make this available to participants who request a copy. We are hoping this research will bring helpful information to Chinese churches in USA, and may help churches to use their resources wisely and efficiently for the Kingdom of God. We sincerely request your participation in this project. It may take ten to twenty-five minutes to answer, depends on your church's mission activities.

You will receive an email with a link which directs you to the online questionnaire in two weeks. We found your church contact information through Immanuel Chinese Christian Network (http://www.immanuel. net/OverseasChurch/), AFC directory and your own church website/

Facebook. We understand that your contact information may be out of date. Thus if you currently are not serving in the position described on your website, please let us know. If you are a secretary or an assistant from your church, please help us to forward this email to one of your pastors or elders (or deacons if your church does not have pastors and elders). If your church prefers not to participate in this survey, please feel free to let us know (zywu@tiu.edu), so two weeks later you will not receive our online questionnaire link. Thank you very much for your cooperation!

If you have any questions about this research please write me directly at zywu@tiu.edu, or if you wish to write my supervisor Dr Priest, you may contact him directly at rpriest@tiu.edu .

In His Grace,
Yi-Chin Jeanne Wu

— — —

敬愛的牧長、教牧同工,

主內平安!

過去數十年來美國神學院針對美國教會的宣教運動做出許多調查與研究,為要將人力、物力更有智慧、果效地為大使命事工擺上。不少華人教會多年來亦積極參與宣教事工,然而針對全美華人教會的宣教運動所做的研究卻相當稀少。因此,我們竭誠邀請貴教會參與全美華人教會宣教概況問卷調查,問卷內容包括支持宣教士或宣教機 構、差派短宣隊、舉辦宣教年會等等。這項研究計畫將由三一福音神學院 (Trinity Evangelical Divinity School) 宣教系教授 Dr Robert Priest 指導, 由華人神學生吳怡瑾執行, 並將成為其畢業論文的一部分。Dr Robert Priest 對於 21 世紀的宣教運動及趨勢有許多研究著作及分析, 所有參與問卷調查的華人教會我們都將願意提供這項研究的結果報告, 歡迎日後向我們索取。希望這份研究能對華人普世宣教有所裨益、幫助神國擴展。我們將在兩周後透過 Email 寄給您一個網上問卷調查的連結, 現在這封信僅為預先邀請、通知。問卷調查視各教會宣教活動不同, 應答時間也不同, 約十分鐘到二十五分鐘。

此外，我們是經由「以馬內利華人基督徒網路」的華人教會名錄（http://www.immanuel.net/OverseasChurch/)，「基督使者協會」（AFC) 的通訊錄，以及貴教會的教會網站或臉書得到您的通訊資料。

若是您的通訊資料有誤，或是您目前不再擔任此職份，煩請告知我們。若您是教會的行政同工或秘書，也請幫我們把這封郵件轉寄給教會其中一位牧師或長老（若貴教會沒有牧師或長老，請轉給執事）。若您的教會不願意參與這份問卷調查，也請回信告知我們(zywu@tiu.edu)，兩周後我們不會透過 Email 寄網上問卷調查的連結給您。謝謝您的參與、幫助！

若您有任何問題、意見，歡迎直接寫信給我：zywu@tiu.edu。若您想和我的指導教授 Dr Priest 聯繫，也可以透過他的電郵聯繫：rpriest@tiu.edu。

敬頌主恩滿溢！

主內，吳怡瑾姊妹敬上

Survey Questionnaire
(in English and Chinese)

General Information 一般資料

1. What is your congregation's current (denominational) affiliation?
請問您的教會是屬於什麼宗派或什麼教會分堂?

☐ a.) 神召會 (The Assemblies of God)

☐ b.) 浸信會系統 (Baptist Church)

☐ c.) 靈糧堂分堂 (Bread of Life Christian Church/ Ling-Liang Tang)

☐ d.) 召會/ 聚會所/ 聚會處 (Christian Assembly/ Local Churches)

☐ e.) 宣道會 (Christian and Missionary Alliance (C & MA))

☐ f.) 台福教會 (Evangelical Formosan Church)

☐ g.) 播道會 (Evangelical Free Church)

☐ h.) 路德宗/ 信義會 (Lutheran Church)

☐ i.) 衛理宗/ 循理會/ 循道會 (Methodist Church)

☐ j.) 改革宗 (Reformed Church)

☐ k.) 長老會 (Presbyterian Church)

☐ l.) 無宗派/跨宗派/獨立教會 (Nondenominational/ inter-denominational/ independent church)

☐ m.) 其他, 請註明 (Other, Please specify) _____

2. Approximately what is the total attendance (adults and children) at your church on a typical weekend for all worship services combined?
您的教會所有的主日崇拜聚會的平均人數大約是多少人? (包括孩童和大人)。

_____

3. In what language do the ministers preach? Please rate the frequency of EACH language:
您的教會主日崇拜用哪些語言講道? 請在下列的選項中標出每一種語言被使用的頻率:

	Never 從來沒有	Several times a year 一年偶爾幾次	Several times a month 一個月偶爾幾次	Once a week 每周一次	Several times a week 每周數次
a. English 英文	☐	☐	☐	☐	☐
b. Mandarin 普通話	☐	☐	☐	☐	☐
c. Cantonese 廣東話	☐	☐	☐	☐	☐
d. Taiwanese 閩南語	☐	☐	☐	☐	☐
e. Spanish 西班牙語	☐	☐	☐	☐	☐
f. Other 其他 _____ (Please specify 請註明)	☐	☐	☐	☐	☐

4. Continue 3. For each language listed above what is the approximate congregation size in your church?
續上題。在上一題中, 您回答了一或多個語言, 而您的教會的會眾大約有多少人在這些不同語言的崇拜聚會? 請回答人數。

a. English英文   _____

b. Mandarin普通話   _____

c. Cantonese廣東話   _____

d. Taiwanese閩南語   _____

e. Spanish西班牙語   _____

f. Other其他_____ (Please specify請註明)   _____

5. Your church is located in 您的教會位於什麼區域?

☐ East coast美國東岸   ☐ Midwest美國中西部   ☐ South美國南方

☐ West coast美國西岸   ☐ Other region其他區域

6. You serve as 您是教會的

☐ Chinese Pastor (including Mandarin, Cantonese, Taiwanese and other Chinese dialects) 中文堂牧師 (包括普通話、粵語、台語等其他家鄉話的牧師)
☐ English Pastor英文堂牧師 ☐ Senior Pastor 主任牧師
☐ Youth Pastor青年牧師 ☐ Elder長老 ☐ Deacon執事
☐ Other position其他 (Please specify請註明) _____

7. Your ethnicity is 您的族裔是

☐ Chinese華人/ 華裔 ☐ Non-Chinese Asian非華人的亞洲人/ 亞裔
☐ Caucasian白種人 ☐ African/ African American非洲人/ 非裔美人
☐ Hispanic or Latino中南美/ 拉丁裔 ☐ Mixed混血
☐ Other 其他 (Please specify請註明) _____

8. You are originally from/ born in 您的出生地? (您是哪裡人?)

☐ a. China (mainland)中國 (大陸) ☐ b. Hong Kong香港
☐ c. Indonesia印尼 ☐ d. Malaysia馬來西亞 ☐ e. Singapore新加坡
☐ f. Taiwan台灣 ☐ g. USA美國
☐ h. Other其他 (Please specify請註明) _____

9. How often, if ever, does your church organize short-term mission trips abroad?
請問您的教會有差派過短宣隊到國外(美國本土以外)嗎? 如果有的話, 差派短宣隊有多頻繁?
☐ Never從來沒有 **(Please jump to the question 26請跳到第26 題)**
☐ One trip every a few years每幾年一次
☐ One trip every year一年一次 ☐ More than one trip a year一年好幾次
☐ Other situation其他情況 (Please specify請說明) _____

The Most Recent Short-Term Mission Trip of Your Church 教會最近一次差派的短宣隊 (上題回答從來沒有者, 請跳到第26 題)

10. How many days did your church's short-term mission teams spend on the most recent mission trip outside the USA? (Days NOT including traveling)
您的教會最近一次派遣的短宣隊在宣教工場待了多少天? (不包括旅行天數) _____days天

11. Considering the most recent mission trip organized and sponsored by your church, which of the following best describes the activity focus of your church's most recent mission trip?

您的教會最近一次派遣的短宣隊, 最主要的事工為何? (單選)

☐ a. Art/ Drama 文藝/ 音樂/ 戲劇表演佈道
☐ b. Building/ Construction/ Repair勞動服務 (幫忙建屋、
　　清理修繕建築物等等)
☐ c. Children's ministries/ VBS兒童事工/ VBS (兒童假期聖經營)
☐ d. Discipleship Training/ Teaching Bible門徒造就、 聖經培訓
☐ e. Education—teaching English 教育—英文教學
☐ f. Education—other (not English) 教育—其他學科
☐ g. Environmental or justice issues 環保或社會公義
☐ h. Evangelism/ Church planting 佈道/ 傳福音/ 拓荒植堂
☐ i. Medical/ Health Care醫療服務
☐ j. Orphanages孤兒院
☐ k. Power Encounter Healing權能醫治釋放
☐ l. Relief and Development救濟、 賑災
☐ m. Sports體育活動、 運動營
☐ n. Vision Trip/ Prayer Walk 異象之旅/ 訪宣/ 行軍禱告
☐ o. Other其他 (Please specify 請註明) ＿＿＿＿＿＿＿＿＿＿＿

12. Continued from last question. What is the secondary focus? (Multiple answers)

續上題。短宣隊的次要、 其他服事項目為何? (可複選)

☐ a. Art/ Drama 文藝/ 音樂/ 戲劇表演佈道
☐ b. Building/ Construction/ Repair勞動服務 (幫忙建屋、
　　清理修繕建築物等等)
☐ c. Children's ministries/ VBS兒童事工/ VBS (兒童假期聖經營)
☐ d. Discipleship Training/ Teaching Bible門徒造就、 聖經培訓
☐ e. Education—teaching English 教育—英文教學
☐ f. Education—other (not English) 教育—其他學科
☐ g. Environmental or justice issues 環保或社會公義
☐ h. Evangelism/ Church planting 佈道/ 傳福音/ 拓荒植堂
☐ i. Medical/ Health Care醫療服務
☐ j. Orphanages孤兒院

☐ k. Power Encounter Healing權能醫治釋放
☐ l. Relief and Development救濟、賑災
☐ m. Sports體育活動、運動營
☐ n. Vision Trip/ Prayer Walk 異象之旅/ 訪宣/ 行軍禱告
☐ o. Other其他 (Please specify 請註明) _____

13. In the most recent mission trip, what were the first languages of the participants of the short-term mission teams of your church? (Multi-answers)
貴教會最近一次差派的短宣隊成員的第一語言 (母語)
是什麼? (可複選)

☐ a. English英文   ☐ b. Mandarin普通話   ☐ c. Cantonese廣東話
☐ d. Taiwanese閩南語   ☐ e. Spanish西班牙語
☐ f. Other其他 (Please specify請註明) _____

14. Continued from last question. In the most recent mission trip, what were the first languages of the local people whom short-term mission teams were serving? (Multi-answers)
續上題。而在宣教工場，短宣隊員所服事的當地人的第一語言 (母語)是什麼? (可複選)

☐ a. English英文   ☐ b. Mandarin普通話   ☐ c. Cantonese廣東話
☐ d. Taiwanese閩南語   ☐ e. Spanish西班牙語
☐ f. Other其他 (Please specify請註明) _____

15. In the most recent mission trip, did your short-term mission teams need interpreters to communicate with the local people whom they were serving?
貴教會最近一次差派的短宣隊，在宣教工場需要翻譯人員才能和所服事的當地人溝通嗎?

☐ Never從來不需要   ☐ Rarely很少需要   ☐ Sometimes有時需要
☐ Often經常需要   ☐ Always總是需要

16. Who have your teams collaborated with in the short-term mission in the most recent mission trip? (Multi-answers)

貴教會最近一次差派的短宣隊，在宣教工場是和哪些人(貴教會以外的人員) 配搭、同工? (可複選)

☐ a. no other people沒有和其他人同工
☐ b. local Chinese Christians from the mission field和宣教工場
　　　當地的華人基督徒同工
☐ c. local non-Chinese Christians from the mission field和宣教工場當
　　　地的非華人基督徒同工
☐ d. Chinese Christians from USA和美國來的華人基督徒同工
☐ e. non-Chinese Christians from USA和美國來的非華人基督徒同工
☐ f. Chinese Christians from other countries和其他國家來的華人基督徒同工
☐ g. non-Chinese Christians from other countries 和其他國家
　　　來的非華人基督徒同工
☐ h. Chinese non-Christians和未信主的華人合作
☐ i. Non-Chinese non-Christians和未信主的非華人合作
☐ j. Other其他 (Please specify 請詳述)＿＿＿＿＿＿＿＿＿＿＿＿＿＿

Short-Term Mission General Info 教會短宣概況

17. Generally speaking, has your church's short-term mission teams returned repeatedly to the same mission field in the past?

總括來說，您的教會是否一再地差派短宣隊回到同一個宣教工場?

☐ Never從來不　☐ Rarely很少　☐ Sometimes有時
☐ Often經常　☐ Always總是

18. How often, if ever, does your congregation's high school youth program organize short-term mission trips abroad?

請問您的教會有組織以青少年 (初中、高中生) 為主的
短宣隊嗎? 多經常?

☐ Never從來沒有　　　　　　☐ One trip every a few years每幾年一次
☐ One trip every year一年一次　☐ More than one trip a year一年好幾次

19. From your estimate approximately how many people from your church have traveled outside the USA in 2012 on a short-term mission trip sponsored by your church?
根據您的粗略估計，您的教會大約有多少人在2012年參加教會差派的海外短宣隊?

_____ persons 人

20. Did your church send short-term mission teams to any of the following regions in 2012? (Check all boxes that apply)
您的教會在2012年有差派海外短宣隊到下列這些洲/ 區域嗎? 請點選所有短宣隊去過的區域。

☐ Africa非洲　　☐ Latin America拉丁美洲　　☐ Asia亞洲
☐ Middle East中東地區　　　☐ Europe歐洲
☐ Oceania (Australia, New Zealand and Pacific islands) 大洋洲 (澳大利亞, 新西蘭, 太平洋島嶼)　　☐ NO沒有

21. Continued from last question. Which countries? (List All. Please specify mainland China, Hong Kong, Macau, Taiwan if applicable)
續上題。請按照您上題的答案，更具體地列舉出短宣隊去到的國家。(注意: 若短宣隊去過中國大陸、香港澳門或台灣，請在答案中把這些地方區分出來。)

Africa非洲　　　　　_____
Latin America拉丁美洲　_____
Asia亞洲　　　　　　_____
Middle East中東地區　　_____
Europe歐洲　　　　　_____
Oceania 大洋洲　　　　_____

22. The primary ministry for the team in these countries/ areas (answered above) is to: (Check one box) 續上題，貴教會的短宣隊在上述這些國家主要所服事的對象是 (單選)

☐ Chinese people (ethnic)華人/ 華裔　　☐ Chinese and Non-Chinese equally
☐ Non-Chinese people 非華人　　　　　華人和非華人都是主要服事對象

23. How many teams did your church send for overseas short-term mission trips in 2012? 2012 年您的教會差派了多少個海外短宣隊?

_____

24. Continued from last question. The majority of these teams were made up of
續上題。請問這些海外短宣隊以什麼年齡層為主體?

☐ Adults only (above 22)成年人為主體 (22歲以上)
☐ College students大學生為主體
☐ Families; mixed generations家庭為主體 (各年齡層都有)
☐ High school youth初中、高中生為主體
☐ Other其他 (Please specify 請註明) _____

25. Which country outside the United States received the **most** short-term missionaries from your church in 2012? (Please specify mainland China, Hong Kong, Macau, Taiwan if applicable)
在2012年您的教會差派最多的海外短宣隊到哪個國家? (注意: 若是中國大陸、香港澳門或台灣, 請在答案中把這些地方區分出來。)

Africa非洲   _____
Latin America拉丁美洲   _____
Asia亞洲   _____
Middle East中東地區   _____
Europe歐洲   _____
Oceania大洋洲   _____

Mission-related activities 與宣教相關的活動

26. How often, if ever, does your church organize a mission conference?
您的教會多久舉辦一次宣教年會?

☐ Never從來沒有過
☐ Once every a few years每幾年舉辦一次
☐ Once every year一年舉辦一次
☐ More than once per year一年舉辦一次以上
☐ Other situation其他情況 (Please explain 請說明)_____

27. No church can address the needs of the whole world. Based on the organized activities of your church, its teaching and preaching, its financial expenditures, and the personal commitments of its pastoral staff, rate the extent which **EACH** of the following is a prioritized concern of your church: 針對這個世代繁多的需要，每一個教會外展事工的重點都不同，根據您的教會所組織的外展活動、牧長的教導與講道、教會的財政支出以及教牧同工個人的擺上，請評估下列各樣事工在您的教會的重要性: (請標記出每一項事工的優先順位)

Priority -->	Lowest 最不重要	Fifth 第五優先	Fourth 第四優先	Third 第三優先	Secondary 第二優先	Top 最優先
a. 非洲的愛滋病問題 HIV/AIDS in Africa	☐	☐	☐	☐	☐	☐
b. 聖經翻譯 Bible Translation	☐	☐	☐	☐	☐	☐
c. 拓荒植堂 Church Planting	☐	☐	☐	☐	☐	☐
d. 穆斯林宣教 Evangelizing the Muslim world	☐	☐	☐	☐	☐	☐
e. 醫療服務宣教 Medical Missions	☐	☐	☐	☐	☐	☐
f. 對華人骨肉之親傳福音 Missions to Chinese	☐	☐	☐	☐	☐	☐
g. 對普世未得之民宣教 Missions to the Unreached	☐	☐	☐	☐	☐	☐
h. 救濟貧窮 Poverty	☐	☐	☐	☐	☐	☐
i. 種族和解 Racial reconciliation	☐	☐	☐	☐	☐	☐
j. 社會公義 Social justice	☐	☐	☐	☐	☐	☐
k. 海外神學教育 Theological Education abroad	☐	☐	☐	☐	☐	☐

28. What is the approximate total dollar amount of the expenditures of your church in support of ministries and needs outside the United States in 2012?

請粗略地估計，在2012年貴教會支持海外各項事工、宣教的支出約為多少美元?

_____ USD

29. What is the approximate total dollar amount of the expenditures of your church (general budget, facilities, salaries, etc. and including all missions giving) in 2012?

請粗略地估計，在2012年貴教會的總支出約為多少美元? (包括一般支出、設備器材、經常費、薪俸、宣教等等)

_____ USD

30. Approximately how many long-term missionaries serving outside the USA does your church support financially?

您的教會大約支持多少位海外長宣宣教士 (在美國本土以外宣教)?

☐ 0 ☐ 1-5 ☐ 6-10 ☐ 11-15 ☐ 16-20 ☐ 21-25 ☐ 26-30 ☐ 31-35
☐ 36-40 ☐ Above 40

31. Continued from last question. In which countries are these missionaries serving? (List all; please specify mainland China, Hong Kong, Macau, Taiwan if applicable)

續上題。這些長宣宣教士在哪些國家服事? (注意: 若宣教士在中國大陸、香港澳門或台灣，請在答案中把這些地方區分出來。)

Africa非洲 _____

Latin America拉丁美洲 _____

Asia亞洲 _____

Middle East中東地區 _____

Europe歐洲 _____

Oceania大洋洲 _____

32. Continued from last question. How many of these missionaries are serving/ reaching out to ethnic Chinese people?
續上題。這些宣教士當中有多少位是在服事華人/ 華裔或向華人/ 華裔傳福音?

☐ None沒有人 ☐ Few很少   ☐ About half大約一半
☐ Most大部分 ☐ All全部

33. Today more and more American congregations have partnership with churches outside the USA. Does your church have a partnership with churches in other countries?
現在越來越多的美國教會和其他國家的教會有合作關係 (partnership)。您的教會和海外的 (美國本土以外) 教會有合作關係嗎?

☐ NO 沒有   ☐ YES有

34. Continued from last question. Could you please describe what kind of partnership it is?
續上題。可否請您描述一下是什麼樣的合作關係 (partnership)?

_____

_____

35. Continued from last question. In which countries does your church partner with other churches? (List all; please specify mainland China, Hong Kong, Macau, Taiwan if applicable)
續上題。是和哪些國家的教會有合作關係 (partnership)? (注意: 若教會位於中國大陸、香港澳門或台灣，請在答案中把這些地方區分出來。)

Africa非洲   _____
Latin America拉丁美洲 _____
Asia亞洲   _____
Middle East中東地區   _____
Europe歐洲   _____
Oceania大洋洲   _____

36. What positive impact on the participants have you observed from short-term mission in your church?

根據您在教會的觀察，短宣對於貴教會的短宣參
與者有哪些正面影響?

_____

_____

37. What negative impact on the participants have you observed from short-term mission in your church?

根據您在教會的觀察，短宣對於貴教會的短宣參
與者有哪些負面影響?

_____

_____

Personal Experiences on STM 您個人的短宣經驗

38. Have you ever been on short-term mission trip outside the USA? If YES, how many times have you ever been on short-term mission trips outside the USA?

您本身有去過美國本土以外的地方短宣嗎? 若有，您去過幾次海
外(美國本土以外) 短宣?

☐ NO沒有   ☐ YES有
                            _____ times次

39. Continued from last question. Which countries have you been to?
(List all; please specify mainland China, Hong Kong, Macau, Taiwan if applicable)

續上題。您去過哪些國家短宣? (注意: 若是去中國大陸、香港澳門
或台灣，請在答案中把這些地方區分出來。)

Africa非洲   _____

Latin America拉丁美洲 _____

Asia亞洲   _____

Middle East中東地區   _____

Europe歐洲   _____

Oceania大洋洲   _____

Thank you so much for your participation! Please be assured that this survey is anonymous. Any information that you provide will be held in strict confidence. At no time will your name be reported along with your response. God bless your ministry!

這份問卷調查到此完全結束。謝謝您的耐心做答! 再次提醒您，這份問卷完全是匿名的，您所有的答案和您的身分都沒有人能夠知道。願神賜福您的事工!

Questionnaire Design

The overall online survey was designed under the page SurveyMonkey, which has a Chinese version (http://zh.surveymonkey.com), and thus the questionnaire was designed both in English and Chinese. The link of the survey was enclosed in an email invitation letter, which has both Chinese and English explanation as well. The whole questionnaire included forty-two items. The first item was language preference. The questions which present the nature of churches, such as size, denominations, etc., are included as well. The next section of questions is focused on the issues related to mission activities, including short-term mission trips. And those more common affiliations are listed.

In this dissertation I build on research carried out by Dr Robert Priest with megachurches (Priest, Wilson, and Johnson) and with Korean American congregations (results not yet published), using nine questions unchanged from his survey, and modifying the response choices slightly on five additional of his survey questions, while adding my own additional questions. That is, at one level this research builds on this prior research, but also moves it in a new direction of exploring diaspora linkages. Since this research intends to make comparisons between US Chinese churches and other churches in the USA, it makes the data symmetrical by adopting some questions of previous questionnaires. This ensures that survey results can be carefully compared with prior survey results of other churches.

There are some questions which are designed for the unique practice of the US Chinese church, for example, the collaboration with other Chinese in the mission field during short-term mission trips (see the question below). Since this research was trying to find how language and ethnicity play an important role in the short-term missions done by US Chinese churches, these questions concerning languages, ethnicity and countries are essential. Also, some other questions are designed to prove that whether there is a preference for Chinese churches' mission investment in missions. The preference could be ethnic groups and countries, for example, the questions concerning the areas where they send STM teams or long-term missionaries. These kinds of questions are also to test the hypotheses of this research.

1.   How often, if ever, does your church organize short-term mission trips abroad?
   (1) Never
   (2) Less than once a year
   (3) Once every year
   (4) More than once a year
   (5) Other (explain):

2.   How many teams did your church send for overseas short-term mission trips in 2012?

3.   Continue the last question. The majority of these teams were made up of:
   (1) Adults only (above 22)
   (2) High school youth
   (3) College students
   (4) Families; mixed generations
   (5) Other (explain):

4.   In the most recent mission trip, what were the first languages of the participants of the short-term mission teams of your church? (Multi-answer)
   (1) English
   (2) Mandarin
   (3) Cantonese
   (4) Taiwanese (Hokkienese)
   (5) Other

5. In the most recent mission trip, what were the first languages of the local people whom short-term mission teams were serving? (Multi-answer)

   (1) English

   (2) Mandarin

   (3) Cantonese

   (4) Taiwanese (Hokkienese)

   (5) Other

6. In the most recent mission trip, did your short-term mission teams need interpreters to communicate with the local people whom they were serving?

   (1) Never

   (2) Rarely

   (3) Sometimes

   (4) Often

   (5) Always

7. Who have your teams collaborated with in the short-term mission in the most recent mission trip? (multi-answer)

   (1) no other people

   (2) local Chinese Christians from the mission field

   (3) local non-Chinese Christians from the mission field

   (4) other Chinese Christians from USA

   (5) other non-Chinese Christians from USA

   (6) other Chinese Christians from other countries

   (7) other non-Chinese Christians from other countries

   (8) Chinese non-Christians

   (9) Non-Chinese non-Christians

8. Has your church sent short-term mission teams to these regions in 2012? (check box)

   (1) Africa

   (2) Latin America

   (3) Asia

   (4) Middle East

   (5) Europe

   (6) Oceania

9. Continued from last question. Which countries? (List all. Please specify mainland China, Hong Kong, Macau, Taiwan if applicable)
   (1) Africa
   (2) Latin America
   (3) Asia
   (4) Middle East
   (5) Europe
   (6) Oceania

10. Continue from last question. Your primary ministry in these countries/ areas (answered above) is to: (check box)
   ☐ Chinese people
   ☐ Non-Chinese people
   ☐ Chinese and non-Chinese equally

11. Which country outside the United States received the most short-term missionaries from your church in 2012? (please specify Mainland China, Hong Kong, Macao, Taiwan if applicable)
   (1) Africa
   (2) Latin America
   (3) Asia
   (4) Middle East
   (5) Europe
   (6) Oceania

12. General speaking, has your church's short-term mission teams returned to the same mission field in the past?
   (1) Never
   (2) Rarely
   (3) Sometimes
   (4) Often
   (5) Always

13. In which countries are these missionaries serving? (List all; please specify mainland China, Hong Kong, Macau, Taiwan if applicable)
   (1) Africa
   (2) Latin America

(3) Asia

(4) Middle East

(5) Europe

(6) Oceania

14. Continued from last question. How many of these missionaries are serving/ reaching out to ethnic Chinese people?

(1) None

(2) Few

(3) About half

(4) Most

(5) All of them

15. Today more and more American congregations have partnership with churches outside the USA. Does your church have a partnership with churches in other countries?

☐ NO

☐ YES

16. Continued from last question. Could you please describe what kind of partnership it is?

17. Continued from last question. In which countries does your church partner with other churches? (List all; please specify mainland China, Hong Kong, Macau, Taiwan if applicable)

(1) Africa

(2) Latin America

(3) Asia

(4) Middle East

(5) Europe

(6) Oceania

18. What positive impact on the participants have you observed from short-term mission in your church?

19. What negative impact on the participants have you observed from short-term mission in your church?

20. Have you ever been on short-term mission trip outside the USA?
   ☐ NO
   ☐ YES

21. Continued from last question. Which countries have you been to?
(List all; please specify mainland China, Hong Kong, Macau, Taiwan if applicable)
   (1) Africa
   (2) Latin America
   (3) Asia
   (4) Middle East
   (5) Europe
   (6) Oceania

22. Wow, you have done lots of short-term mission trips! Would you consider being interviewed by us and share about your short-term mission experiences? If YES, please give us your contact info here, or send to this email: zywu@tiu.edu
   ☐ NO
   ☐ YES – Your contact info: _____

In sum, nine items of this questionnaire are directly adopted from the survey of Priest et al. (2010), five are adopted with adjustment, and twenty-seven are designed particularly for this research. The questionnaire is mainly designed to answer these questions: the countries to which overseas Chinese churches are sending short-term mission teams, what kind of people they are sending, what kind of mission work they are doing in the mission field for their mission trips, and how many resources, where, and to whom they invest in overseas missions. Some of the questions are querying for facts, not for measuring. For example:

> In the most recent mission trip, what were the first languages of participants of the short-term mission teams of your church? (Multi-answer)
>
> (1) English
> (2) Mandarin
> (3) Cantonese

(4) Taiwanese (Hokkienese)
(5) Spanish
(6) Other

But some other questions related to frequency or intensity are designed to measure the level. For example:

Has your church's short-term mission teams returned to the same mission field?

(1) Never
(2) Rarely
(3) Sometimes
(4) Often
(5) Always

And there are three open descriptive questions for respondents to share their experiences and comments. For example:

What positive impact on the participants have you observed from short-term mission in your church?

Interview Questions

The purposes and goals of the interviews were: (1) to gather more in-depth data and perspectives from pastors who are very experienced in short-term mission (since the questionnaire only collects general quantitative data), (2) to compare with the result of quantitative research data and determine if there is any consistency or contradiction, and (3) to find the reason why Chinese churches in the USA send short-term mission teams to mostly Chinese (if proven by the quantitative data).

1) Could you please explain to me the vision and goal of the outreach and evangelistic ministries and mission activities of your church?

2) Please describe to me how your church runs STM, e.g. how many short-term mission teams are sent every year, what is the size of the team, where they are going, what their tasks are, how funds are raised, etc.

3) Who are going to STM trips, and what is the requirement of being a short-term mission team member?

4) Please tell me the reasons your church chose to send short-term mission teams to these countries.

5) What is the relation between your church and the receiving or hosting church/people? Do you have any partnership or relationship like sister churches or from the same denomination?

6) What is the response of the receiving or hosting church/people?

7) What is the feedback of the short-term mission participants?

8) How are these mission trips effective or ineffective? In which way?

9) From your observation is STM helpful for the STM-goers and the church to have more knowledge and acceptance of other cultures and cross-cultural ministries? In which way?

10) Through the survey we found that most Chinese churches are sending short-term mission teams to Chinese people in other area. What possible reasons could it be?

11) Do you have other comments or insights related to short-term mission or missions that you would like to share with us?

Informed Consent Form

Dear Church Leader,

Greetings in the name of our Lord Jesus Christ!

My name is Yi-Chin Jeanne Wu, currently a PhD student in Trinity Evangelical Divinity School. Recently, I am writing my dissertation related to the mission movement of Chinese churches in the USA. In order to conduct this research, I need to interview a few Chinese church leaders in the USA. I am writing to humbly request for your participation in this interview. It will take about 30 to 60 minutes to answer these questions. If you are interested in the research results, please feel free to contact me as well. Please be assured that any information that you provide will be held in strict confidence. At no time will your name be reported along with your response. Please understand that your participation in this research is totally voluntary and you are free to withdraw at any time during this study. Thank you very much for your help!

May the Lord bless the work of your hands!

In His Grace,
Yi-Chin Jeanne Wu

Please read and sign below:

"I acknowledge that I have been informed of, and understand, the nature and purpose of this study, and I freely consent to participate."

Name_____ Signed_____ Date_____

Bibliography

Adeney, Miriam. "When the Elephant Dances, the Mouse May Die." In *Short-Term Missions Today,* edited by Bill Berry, 86–89. Pasadena, CA: Into All the World Magazine, 2003.

———. "Shalom Tourist: Loving Your Neighbor While Using Her." *Missiology* 34, no. 4 (2006): 463–476.

———. "The Myth of the Blank Slate: A Check-List for Short-Term Missions." In *Effective Engagement in Short-Term Missions: Doing It Right!,* edited by Robert Priest, 121–145. Pasadena, CA: William Carey Library, 2008.

———. "Being There: Short-Term Missions and Human Need." Paper presented at Evangelical Missiological Society Regional Meeting, 30 July – 1 August 2009, hosted by Carl F. H. Henry Center, Trinity Evangelical Divinity School, 2009.

Adkins, Julie. "Beyond Development and 'Projects': The Globalization of Solidarity." In *Bridging the Gaps: Faith-Based Organizations, Neoliberalism, and Development in Latin America and the Caribbean*, edited by Tara Hefferan, Julie Adkins, and Laurie Occhipinti, 103–118. Lanham, MD: Rowman and Littlefield, 2009.

Ambassador for Christ International. Chinese Church and Organization Directory. 2012. *OursWeb.* http://church.oursweb.net/slocation.php?w=5&c= US&a=&t= (accessed 17 November 2012).

Amersfoort, Hans van. "Gabriel Sheffer and the Diaspora Experience." *Diaspora: A Journal of Transnational Studies* 13, no. 2/3 (2004): 359–373.

Babbie, Earl. *The Practice of Social Research.* 11th ed. Belmont, CA: Wadsworth, 2007.

Barrett, David, Todd M. Johnson, and Peter F. Crossing. "Missiometrics 2005: A Global Survey of World Mission." *International Bulletin of Missionary Research* 29, no. 1 (2005): 27–30.

Barrett, David, and Todd Johnson. *World Christian Trends, AD 30-AD 2200: Interpreting the Annual Christian Megacensus.* Pasadena, CA: William Carey Library, 2001.

Berger, Peter. *The Sacred Canopy.* Garden City, NY: Doubleday Anchor, 1969.

Bernard, H. Russell. *Research Methods in Anthropology*. Lanham, MD: Altamira, 2011.

Besley, A. C. "Hybridized and Globalized: Youth Cultures in the Postmodern Era." *The Review of Education, Pedagogy, and Cultural Studies* 25 (2003): 153–177.

Beyerlein, K. G. Adler, and J. Trinitapoli. "The Effect of Religious Short-Term Mission Trips on Youth Civic Engagement." *Journal for the Scientific Study of Religion* 50, no. 4 (2011): 780–795.

Birth, Kevin. "What Is Your Mission Here? A Trinidadian Perspective on Visits from the 'Church of Disneyworld'." *Missiology* 34, no. 4 (2006): 497–508.

Blomberg, Fran. "From 'Whatever' to Wherever: Enhancing Faith Formation in Young Adults through Short-Term Missions." In *Effective Engagement in Short-Term Missions: Doing It Right!*, edited by Robert Priest, 591–611. Pasadena, CA: William Carey Library, 2008.

Brown, C. M. "Friendship Is Forever: Congregation-to-Congregation Relationships." In *Effective Engagement in Short-Term Missions: Doing It Right!*, edited by Robert Priest, 203–231. Pasadena, CA: William Carey Library, 2008.

Butler, Kim D. "Defining Diaspora, Refining a Discourse." *Diaspora* 10, no. 2 (2001): 189–219.

Carnes, Tony, and Fenggang Yang, eds. *Asian American Religions: The Making and Remaking of Border and Boundaries*. New York, NY: New York University Press, 2004.

Cao, Nanlai. *Constructing China's Jerusalem: Christians, Power, and Place in Contemporary Wenzhou*. Stanford, CA: Stanford University Press, 2011.

Carpenter, Mary Yeo. "Familism and Ancestor Veneration: A Look at Chinese Funeral Rites." *Missiology: An International Review* 24, no. 4 (1996): 503–517.

Cartier, Carolyn. "Diaspora and Social Restructuring in Postcolonial Malaysia." In *The Chinese Diaspora: Space, Place, Mobility, and Identity*, edited by J. C. Ma and Carolyn Cartier, 69–96. Lanham, MD: Roman & Littlefield, 2003.

Casino, Tereso C. "Why People Move? A Prolegomenon to Diaspora Missiology." In *Korean Diaspora and Christian Mission*, edited by S. Hun Kim and Wonsuk Ma, 35–58. Eugene, OR: Wipf and Stock, 2011.

CCCOWE. "Our History." *CCCOWE website*. http://www.cccowe.org/content.php?id=about_history_chart (accessed 12 April 2014).

———. "The Statistics Data of Overseas Chinese Population and Chinese Church." *Chinese Church Today* (今日華人教會). Hong Kong: Chinese Coordination Centre of World Evangelism, no. 281 (2011): 8–10.

———. "An Introduction." *CCCOWE website*. 2013. http://www.cccowe.org/content.php?id=about_cccowe_movement_brief (accessed 12 April 2014).

Chai, Andrew. "Short-Term Missions: Do You Take It Seriously?" (短宣: 你是認真的嗎?) *Gospel Operation International* (華傳), 21 (May–June 2013). http://gointl.org/gointl_portal/publication/magazine/article/1574

Chan, Kim-Kong. "Case Study 2: Missiological Implications of Chinese Christians in Diaspora." In *Diaspora Missiology: Theory, Methodology, and Practice*, edited by Enoch Wan, 181–197. Portland, OR: Institute of Diaspora Studies-USA, 2011.

Chen, Tzeng-Ching. "Challenge and Solution: A Discussion on Chinese Church in North America" (挑戰與因應之道——論北美華人教會), Ambassadors Magazine (使者雜誌), 9/10 (1997), http://soareagle55. wordpress.com/2008/10/26, (accessed 1 October 2010).

Chen, Zhongping. "Building the Chinese Diaspora across Canada: Chinese Diasporic Discourse and the Case of Peterborough, Ontario." *Diaspora* 13, no. 2/3 (2007): 185–210.

Chinese Christian Herald Crusades. Church directory. 2012. http://cchcherald. org/us/?page_id=49 (accessed 17 November 2012).

Chuang, Tsu-Kung. 2007. "It Is Time to Reflect: Rethink the Mission Strategy of Chinese Church" (該是檢討的時候了——華人教會宣教策略的省思). *Church China* (教會), issue 8, November. https://www.churchchina. org/?q=no071101 (accessed 14 March 2014).

Clifford, James. "Diasporas." *Cultural Anthropology* 9, no. 3 (1994): 302–338.

Cohen, Robin. *Global Diasporas: An Introduction*. Seattle, WA: University of Washington Press, 1997.

Decker, Murray S. "Student Sojourners and Spiritual Formation: Understanding the Intersection of Cross-Cultural Adjustment and Spiritual Disorientation." In *Effective Engagement in Short-Term Missions: Doing It Right!*, edited by Robert Priest, 559–590. Pasadena, CA: William Carey Library, 2008.

De Vos, George. *Ethnic Identity: Creation, Conflict and Accommodation*. Walnut Creek, CA: Altamira, 1995.

Dufoix, Stéphane. *Diasporas*. Berkeley, CA: University of California Press, 2008.

EMIS. Mission Handbook: U.S. and Canadian Protestant Ministries Overseas. 21st ed. Monrovia, CA: MARC, 2010.

Eitzen, Martín Hartwig. "Short-Term Missions: A Latin American Perspective." *Journal of Latin American Theology: Christian Reflections from the Latino South* 2 (2007): 33–47. (Special issue on short-term missions in Latin America, with guest editors Robert Priest and Tito Paredes.)

Escobar, Samuel. "Migration: Avenue and Challenge to Mission." *Missiology* 31, no. 1 (2003): 17–28.

Fan, C. Cindy. "Chinese Americans: Immigration, Settlement, and Social Geography." In *The Chinese Diaspora: Space, Place, Mobility, and Identity*, edited by J. C. Ma and Carolyn Cartier, 261–291. Lanham, MD: Roman & Littlefield, 2003.

FlorCruz, Jaimes. "China's Urban Population Outnumbers Rural Dwellers for the First Time." 2012. http://www.cnn.com/2012/01/17/world/asia/china-urban-population-duplicate-2/index.html?hpt=wo_bn4 (accessed 6 January 2014).

Foley, Michael, and Dean Hoge. *Religion and the New Immigrants*. New York, NY: Oxford University Press, 2007.

Garrison, David. *A Wind in the House of Islam*. Monument, CO: WIGTake, 2014.

Glasser, Arthur F., with Charles E. Van Engen, Dean S. Gilliland, and Shawn B. Redford. *Announcing the Kingdom: The Story of God's Mission in the Bible*. Grand Rapids, MI: Baker, 2003.

Godley, Michael R. *The Mandarin-Capitalists from Nanyang*. Cambridge: Cambridge University Press, 1981.

Gold, Thomas, Doug Guthrie, and David Wank. *Social Connection in China: Institutions, Culture, and the Changing Nature of Guanxi*. Cambridge: Cambridge University Press, 2002.

Hale, Thomas. *On Being a Missionary*. Pasadena, CA: William Carey Library, 1995.

Hamlin, Kevin, and Li Yanping. "China Overtakes Japan as the World's Second Biggest Economy." *Bloomberg News*, 16 August 2010. http://www.bloomberg.com/ news/2010-08-16/china-economy-passes-japan-s-in-second-quarter-cappingthree-decade-rise.html (accessed 6 January 2014).

Hanciles, Jehu J. *Beyond Christendom: Globalization, African Migration and the Transformation of the West*. Maryknoll, NY: Orbis Books, 2008.

Hartford Institute for Religion Research. "Fast Facts about American Religion." 2000–2006. http://hirr.hartsem.edu/research/fastfacts/fast_facts.html#sizecong (accessed 14 April 2014).

Hiebert, Paul. "The Missionary as Mediator of Global Theologizing." In *Globalizing Theology: Belief and Practice in an Era of World Christianity*, edited by Craig Ott and Harold A. Netland, 288–308. Grand Rapids, MI: Baker, 2006.

Holton, Robert J. *Making Globalization*. New York, NY: Palgrave Macmillan, 2005.

———. *Global Networks*. New York, NY: Palgrave Macmillan, 2008.

Hong Kong Bible Society. "About Us." *Hong Kong Bible Society Website*. 2014. http://www.hkbs.org.hk/tw/content/10-about-6 (accessed 15 April 2014).

Hong, Sokpyo. "The Impact of Short-Term Mission Trips on Interracial and Interethnic Attitudes among Korean American Church Members." PhD diss., Trinity International University, 2011.

Immanuel Christian Chinese Network. "Overseas Chinese Church Directory." 2012. http://www.immanuel.net/OverseasChurch (accessed 17 November 2012).

International Monetary Fund. "World Economic Outlook Databases." *International Monetary Fund Website*. 2012. http://www.imf.org/external/ns/cs.aspx?id=28 (accessed 12 April 2014).

Jandt, F. E. *An Introduction to Intercultural Communication: Identities in a Global Community*. 6th ed. Thousand Oaks, CA: Sage, 2007.

Johnstone, David M. "Closing the Loop: Debriefing and the Short-Term College Missions Team." *Missiology* 34, no. 4 (2006): 523–529.

Johnstone, Patrick, and Mandryk, Jason. *Operation World*. Colorado Springs, CO: Global Mapping International, 2001.

Kim, S. Hun, and Wonsuk Ma, eds. *Korean Diaspora and Christian Mission*. Eugene, OR: Wipf and Stock Publishers, 2011.

Kjeldgaard, Dannie, and Søren Askegaard. "The Glocalization of Youth Culture: The Global Youth Segment as Structures of Common Difference." *Journal of Consumer Research* 33, no. 2 (2006): 231–247.

Lam, Wan Shun Eva. "Border Discourses and Identities in Transnational Youth Culture." In *What They Don't Learn in School: Literacy in the Lives of Urban Youth*, edited by Jabari Mahiri, 1–16. New York: Peter Lang, 2004.

Levinskaya, Irina. *The Book of Acts in Its Diaspora Setting*. The Book of Acts in Its First Century Setting, Vol. 5. Grand Rapids, MI: Eerdmans, 1996.

Li, Xisuo (李喜所). 梁啟超是提出"中華民族"稱謂的第一人. 人民網. 2006. http://theory.people.com.cn/BIG5/49157/49163/4089792.html (accessed 22 February 2014).

Lien, Pei-te, and Tony Carnes. "The Religious Demography of Asian Boundary Crossing." In *Asian American Religions: The Making and Remaking of Border and Boundaries*, edited by Tony Carnes and Fenggang Yang, 38–54. New York, NY: New York University Press, 2004.

Ling, Samuel. *The "Chinese Way" of Doing Things: Perspective on American-Born Chinese and the Chinese Church in North America*. San Gabriel: China Horizon, 1999.

Linhart, Terence David. "They Were So Alive! The Spectacle Self and Youth Group Short-Term Mission Trips." *Missiology* 34, no. 4 (2006): 451–462.

Ma, Ringo. "Communication Experiences and Adaptation of Mainland Chinese in Hong Kong and Hong Kong Chinese in Mainland China." *Journal of Intercultural Communication Research* 38, no. 2 (2009): 115–132.

Ma, Laurence J. C. "Space, Place and Transnationalism in the Chinese Diaspora." In *The Chinese Diaspora: Space, Place, Mobility, and Identity*, edited by J. C. Ma and Carolyn Cartier, 1–49. Lanham, MD: Roman & Littlefield, 2003.

Ma, Laurence J. C., and Carolyn Cartier, eds. *The Chinese Diaspora: Space, Place, Mobility, and Identity*. Lanham, MD: Roman & Littlefield, 2003.

Mandryk, Jason. *Operation World*. 7th ed. Colorado Springs, CO: Biblica, 2010.

Maslucán, Rodrigo. "Short-Term Missions: Analysis and Proposals." In *Journal of Latin American Theology: Christian Reflections from the Latino South* 2: (2007): 139–158. (Special issue on short-term missions in Latin America, with guest editors Robert Priest and Tito Paredes.)

MacDonald, G. Jefferey. "Rise of Sunshine Samaritans: On a Mission of Holiday?" *The Christian Science Monitor*, 25 May 2006.

McKeown, Adam. "Ethnographies of Chinese Transnationalism." *Diaspora* 10, no. 3 (2001): 341–360.

Moreau, A. Scott. "Short-Term Missions in the Context of Missions, Inc." In *Effective Engagement in Short-Term Missions: Doing It Right!*, edited by Robert Priest, 1–33. Pasadena, CA: William Carey Library, 2008.

Morgan, George A., Nancy L. Leech, Gene W. Gloeckner, Karen C. Barrett. *SPSS for Introductory Statistics: Use and Interpretation*. 3rd ed. Mahwah, NJ: Lawrence Erlbaum, 2007.

National Congregations Study (NCS). National Congregations Study website. 2010. http://www.soc.duke.edu/natcong/ (accessed 12 April 2014).

Nayak, Anoop. Race, Place and Globalization: Youth Cultures in a Changing World. Oxford: Berg, 2003.

Neill, Stephen. A History of Christian Missions. 2nd ed. New York, NY: Penguin Books, 1991.

Offutt, Stephen. "The Role of Short-Term Mission Teams in the New Centers of Global Christianity." Journal for the Scientific Study of Religion 50, no. 4 (2011): 796–811.

Osaghae, Eghosa. "On the Concept of the Ethnic Group in Africa: A Nigeria Case." Plural Societies XVI, no. 2 (1986): 77–88.

Pan, Lynn, ed. *The Encyclopedia of the Chinese Overseas*. 2nd ed. Singapore: Editions Didier Millet, 2006.

Pantoja Jr, Luis, Sadiri Joy Tira, and Enoch Wan, eds. *Scattered: The Filipino Global Presence*. Manila, Philippines: LifeChange, 2004.

Park, Kyeong-Sook. "Researching Short-Term Missions and Paternalism." In *Effective Engagement in Short-Term Missions: Doing It Right!*, edited by Robert Priest, 499–522. Pasadena, CA: William Carey Library, 2008.

Parker, David. "Going with the Flow?: Reflections on Recent Chinese Diaspora Studies." *Diaspora* 14, no. 2/3 (2009): 411–423.

Payne, J. D. *Strangers Next Door: Immigration, Migration and Mission*. Downers Grove, IL: InterVarsity, 2012.

Peng, Shiyong. Culture and Conflict Management in Foreign-Invested Enterprises in China. Bern: Peter Lang, 2003.

People's Daily. 人民日报：外资并未大规模撤离中国. 2013. http://news. xinhuanet.com/fortune/2013-08/12/c_125151151.htm (accessed 14 April 2013).

Peterson, Roger, Gordon Aeschliman, R. Wayne Sneed. Maximum Impact Short-Term Mission: The God-Commanded, Repetitive Deployment of Swift, Temporary, Non-Professional Missionaries. Minneapolis, MN: STEM, 2003.

Priest, Robert J., Terry Dischinger, Steve Rasmussen, and C. M. Brown. "Researching the Short-Term Mission Movement." Missiology 34, no. 4 (2006): 431–450.

Priest, Robert J., ed. Effective Engagement in Short-Term Missions: Doing It Right! Pasadena, CA: William Carey Library, 2008.

———. "Short-Term Mission as a New Paradigm." In Mission after Christendom: Emergent Themes in Contemporary Mission, edited by Ogbu Kalu, Peter Vethanayagamony, and Edmund Kee-Fook Chia, 84–99. Louisville, KT: Westminster John Knox, 2010.

Priest, Robert J., Douglas Wilson, and Adelle Johnson. "U.S. Megachurches and New Patterns of Global Mission." International Bulletin of Missionary Research 34, no. 2 (2010): 97–104.

Richardson, Rick. "The Impact of Urban Short-Term Projects on the Social Connections of Evangelical College Students." In Effective Engagement in Short-Term Missions: Doing It Right!, edited by Robert Priest, 525–550. Pasadena, CA: William Carey Library, 2008.

Ro, Jonathan. "Globalization's Impact on the Urban Church in China: A Multiple Case-Study of Four Churches in a Major Urban Center." PhD diss., Trinity International University, 2013.

Royle, Marjorie H., and Destiny Shellhammer. "Potential Response Bias in Internet Use for Survey Religious Research." Reviews of Religious Research 49, no. 1 (2007): 54–68.

Rutgers, L. V. The Hidden Heritage of Diaspora Judaism. 2nd ed. Bondgenotenlaan, Belgium: Uitgeveij Peeters, 1998.

Safran, William. "Diasporas in Modern Societies: Myths of Homeland and Return." Diaspora 1, no. 1 (1991): 83–99.

Sassen, Saskia. A Sociology of Globalization. New York, NY: W. W. Norton & Company, 2007.

Schiller, Nina Glick, Linda Basch, and Cristina Blanc-Szanton, eds. Towards a Transnational Perspective on Migration: Race, Class, Ethnicity, and Nationalism Reconsidered. New York, NY: New York Academy of Sciences, 1992.

Sheffer, Gabriel. "A File of Study: Modern Diasporas in International Politics." In Modern Diaspora in International Politics, edited by Gabriel Sheffer, 36–61. London: Croom Helm, 1986.

————. *Diaspora Politics: At Home Abroad.* Cambridge, UK: Cambridge University Press, 2003.

————. "Transnationalism and Ethnonational Diasporism." *Diaspora* 15, no. 1 (2006): 121–145.

Shim, Doobo. "Hybridity and the Rise of Korean Popular Culture in Asia." *Media, Culture & Society* 28, no. 1 (2006): 25–44.

Slimbach, Richard. "The Mindful Missioner." In *Effective Engagement in Short-Term Missions: Doing It Right!*, edited by Robert Priest, 147–177. Pasadena, CA: William Carey Library, 2008.

Stott, John R. W. *Christian Mission in the Modern World.* Downers Grove, IL: InterVarsity, 1975.

Thumma, Scott. "Virtually Religious: Technology and Internet Use in American Congregations." *Faith Communities Today: American Congregations 2010.* 2010. http://faithcommunitiestoday.org/sites/faithcommunitiestoday.org/files/Techno logy-Internet-Use.pdf (accessed 14 April 2014).

Tong, Chee-Kiong, and Chan Kwok-bun. "One Face, Many Masks: The Singularity and Plurality Chinese Identity." *Diaspora* 10, no. 3 (2001): 361–389.

Tong, Joy Kooi-Chin. *Overseas Chinese Christian Entrepreneurs in Modern China: A Case Study of Christian Ethics on Business Life.* London: Anthem, 2012.

Tölölyan, Khachig. "Rethinking Diaspora(s): Stateless Power in the Transnational Moment." *Diaspora* 6, no.1 (1996): 3–36.

Trinitapoli, Jenny, and Stephen Vaisey. "The Transformative Role of Religious Experience: The Case of Short-Term Missions." *Social Forces* 88, no. 1 (2009): 121–146.

U. N. Department of Economic and Social Affairs. "World Population Prospects: The 2010 Revision: Highlights and Advance Tables." Global Migration Group. New York: United Nations, 2011. http://esa.un.org/unpd/wpp/Documentation/pdf/WPP2012_ HIGHLIGHTS.pdf (accessed 14 April 2014).

United States Census Bureau. "The Foreign-Born Population of the United States." 2010. http://www.census.gov/newsroom/pdf/cspan_fb_slides.pdf (accessed 14 April 2014).

————. "The Asian Population: 2010." Office of Immigration Statistics 2012. http://www.census.gov/prod/cen2010/briefs/c2010br-11.pdf (accessed 14 April 2014).

Van Engen, Charles. *Mission on the Way: Issues in Mission Theology.* Grand Rapids, MI: Baker, 1996.

Van Hear, Nicholas. *New Diasporas: The Mass Exodus, Dispersal and Regrouping of Migrant Communities.* Seattle, WA: University of Washington Press, 1998.

Ver Beek, Kurt. "International Service-Learning: A Call to Caution." In *Commitment and Connection: Service-Learning and Christian Higher Education*, edited by Gail Gunst Heffner and Claudia DeVries Beversluis, 55–69. New York, NY: University Press of America, 2002.

———. "The Impact of Short-Term Missions: A Case Study of House Construction in Honduras after Hurricane Mitch." *Missiology* 34, no. 4 (2006): 477–495.

———. "Lessons from the Sapling: Review of Quantitative Research on Short-Term Missions." In *Effective Engagement in Short-Term Missions: Doing It Right!*, edited by Robert Priest, 469–496. Pasadena, CA: William Carey Library, 2008.

Villon, Joaquin Alegre. "Short-Term Missions: Experiences and Perspectives from Callao, Peru." *Journal of Latin American Theology: Christian Reflections from the Latino South* 2 (2007): 119–138. (Special issue on short-term missions in Latin America, with guest editors Robert Priest and Tito Paredes.)

Walls, Andrew. *The Missionary Movement in Christian History: Studies in the Transmission of Faith*. Maryknoll, NY: Orbis, 1996.

Wan, Enoch. "Mission among the Chinese Diaspora: A Case Study of Migration & Mission." *Missiology* XXXI, no. 1 (2003): 35–43.

———. "Diaspora Missiology." *EMS*, Occasional Bulletin (2008): 3–7.

———, ed. *Diaspora Missiology: Theory, Methodology, and Practice*. Portland, OR: Institute of Diaspora Studies-USA, 2011.

Wan, Enoch, and Geoffrey Hartt. "Complementary Aspects of Short-Term Missions and Long-Term Missions: Case Studies for a Win-Win Situation." In *Effective Engagement in Short-Term Missions: Doing It Right!*, edited by Robert Priest, 63–100. Pasadena, CA: William Carey Library, 2008.

Wan, Enoch, and Sadiri Joy Tira. "Diaspora Missiology." In *Missions Practice in the 21st Century*, edited by Enoch Wan and Sadiri Joy Tira, 27–54. Pasadena, CA: William Carey University Press, 2009.

Wang, Chin T. (John). "Urban Church Resources for Short-Term Mission." In *Effective Engagement in Short-Term Missions: Doing It Right!*, edited by Robert Priest, 233–249. Pasadena, CA: William Carey Library, 2008.

———. "Immigrant Churches and Their Mission: A Comparative Study of the Mission Practices among the Chinese, Hispanic, and African Immigrant Churches in New York City." PhD diss., Trinity International University, 2013.

Wang, Gungwu. *China and the Chinese Overseas*. Singapore: Times Academic Press, 1991.

Wang, Yuting, and Fenggang Yang. "More than Evangelical and Ethnic: The Ecological Factor in Chinese Conversion to Christianity in the United States." *Sociology of Religion* 67, no. 2 (2006): 179–192.

Winter, Ralph D., and Steve C. Hawthorne. *Perspectives on the World Christian Movement*. Pasadena, CA: William Carey Library, 1999.

Wuthnow, Robert, and Stephen Offutt. "Transnational Religious Connections." *Sociology of Religion* 69 (2008): 209–232.

Wuthnow, Robert. *Boundless Faith: The Global Outreach of American Churches*. Berkeley, CA: University of California Press, 2009.

Yang, Fenggang. "Chinese Conversion to Evangelical Christianity: The Importance of Social and Cultural Contexts." *Sociology of Religion* 59 (1998): 237–257.

———. *Chinese Christians in America: Conversion, Assimilation, and Adhesive Identities*. University Park, PA: The Penn State University Press, 1999.

———. "Chinese Christian Transnationalism: Diverse Networks of a Houston Church." In *Religions across Borders: Transnational Religious Networks*, edited by Helen Rose Ebaugh and Janet S. Chafetz, 129–148. Walnut Creek, CA: AltaMira, 2002.

———. "Gender and Generation in a Chinese Christian Church." In *Asian American Religions: The Making and Remaking of Border and Boundaries*, edited by Tony Carnes and Fenggang Yang, 205–222. New York, NY: New York University Press, 2004.

———. *Religion in China: Survival and Revival under Communist Rule*. New York, NY: Oxford University Press, 2012.

Yu, Zephaniah T. C. "From the End of Earth to Our Neighbor (從天涯至毗鄰)." *Gospel Operation International* (華傳) 23 (Sept-Oct 2013): 1–3.

Zehner, Edwin. "Short-Term Missions: Toward a More Field-Oriented Model." *Missiology* 34, no. 4 (2006): 509–521.

———. "On the Rhetoric of the Short-Term Missions Appeals: With Some Practical Suggestions for Team Leaders." In *Effective Engagement in Short-Term Missions: Doing It Right!*, edited by Robert Priest, 179–201. Pasadena, CA: William Carey Library, 2008.

Langham Literature and its imprints are a ministry of Langham Partnership.

Langham Partnership is a global fellowship working in pursuit of the vision God entrusted to its founder John Stott –

> *to facilitate the growth of the church in maturity and Christ-likeness through raising the standards of biblical preaching and teaching.*

Our vision is to see churches in the majority world equipped for mission and growing to maturity in Christ through the ministry of pastors and leaders who believe, teach and live by the Word of God.

Our mission is to strengthen the ministry of the Word of God through:

- nurturing national movements for biblical preaching
- fostering the creation and distribution of evangelical literature
- enhancing evangelical theological education

especially in countries where churches are under-resourced.

Our ministry

Langham Preaching partners with national leaders to nurture indigenous biblical preaching movements for pastors and lay preachers all around the world. With the support of a team of trainers from many countries, a multi-level programme of seminars provides practical training, and is followed by a programme for training local facilitators. Local preachers' groups and national and regional networks ensure continuity and ongoing development, seeking to build vigorous movements committed to Bible exposition.

Langham Literature provides majority world preachers, scholars and seminary libraries with evangelical books and electronic resources through publishing and distribution, grants and discounts. The programme also fosters the creation of indigenous evangelical books in many languages, through writer's grants, strengthening local evangelical publishing houses, and investment in major regional literature projects, such as one volume Bible commentaries like *The Africa Bible Commentary* and *The South Asia Bible Commentary*.

Langham Scholars provides financial support for evangelical doctoral students from the majority world so that, when they return home, they may train pastors and other Christian leaders with sound, biblical and theological teaching. This programme equips those who equip others. Langham Scholars also works in partnership with majority world seminaries in strengthening evangelical theological education. A growing number of Langham Scholars study in high quality doctoral programmes in the majority world itself. As well as teaching the next generation of pastors, graduated Langham Scholars exercise significant influence through their writing and leadership.

To learn more about Langham Partnership and the work we do visit **langham.org**

www.ingramcontent.com/pod-product-compliance
Lightning Source LLC
Chambersburg PA
CBHW070326270326
41926CB00017B/3784